DARE TO HOPE

DARE TO
HOPE:
SAVING AMERICAN
DEMOCRACY

Jason West
with
Susan Bell

miramax books

HYPERION

NEW YORK

ISBN 1-4013-5238-3

First Edition
10   9   8   7   6   5   4   3   2   1

*To the thousands of activists who've
made this world a better place,
whose names we'll never know.*

Contents

DARE TO HOPE

Introduction

Most Americans don't vote. We're told that we don't vote because we're apathetic, or because we're so happy with the way things are that we don't see the need.

It's neither.

We don't vote because there's often no point. In most places in America, elections have been decided before a single vote is cast, since district lines are drawn to make sure a Democrat always wins in this district, a Republican in that one. Then there's the money. Unless you've got it, you don't win the office. It costs around a million dollars to win a seat in Congress and five million for one in the Senate. So our politicians are either rich enough to finance their own campaigns, or they're taking money from the very corporations they're sent to Washington to regulate. It's a sad state of democracy when we have to rely on the independently wealthy to bring independent voices to public office.

Our present political system has set itself up as a for-profit enterprise: corporations purchase candidates from both major parties as a business investment. And politicians of both parties deliver. Since candidates work for corporations, not for us, our vote more or less doesn't matter, so why should we bother? Faced with two candidates who say much the same thing, why should we waste our time? Neither party cares about passing laws that would make a better world for us, the nonwealthy majority of Americans—one where there's no need to send our sons and daughters to die for an oil company's profit, where everyone has health care, where jobs are interesting and pay well, where a good education is free, where tolerance reigns, where we can raise kids and build communities that are safe, comfortable, and fun. When we don't vote, it's because we're smart enough to see through the candidates' bullshit.

Platitudes about health care, jobs, and education are a part of every politician's election year speech-making. But more important than what a politician says is what he does. All politicians talk about a better world, but what they do almost always makes things worse for us and better for corporations and the rich. Politicians continually send us into wars that make big businesses richer; they sign away our human rights, send our good jobs to Mexico and China, and leave behind poverty, drugs, and violence in our cities. Politicians have lied to us for years; why should we ever vote for one again?

Both Democrats and Republicans have shown a brazen disregard for what we, the people, want. Did Bill Clinton, a Democratic hero for many, give us a better health care system? He said he would. But with Democratic control of the White House and Congress, what we got was a for-profit HMO system that refuses to treat people who are very sick because it's too expensive. Clinton also gave us the WTO and NAFTA, shipping good-paying union jobs out of the country, and he gave us corporate media mergers. But he said he was for creating jobs at home and for competition in the marketplace. Is George W. Bush the compassionate, moral conservative he claims? He said he'd only send us to war as a last resort, he said that catching bin Laden was his top priority, he said he's fiscally responsible, he said government should stay out of people's lives. Then he sent us into war in Iraq when arms inspectors were making progress, left Osama bin Laden to roam free, created a huge deficit, and gutted the Bill of Rights with the Patriot Act. He never got around to handing over the bulk of the money to his "No Child Left Behind" program. The program itself is set up to test kids instead of improve classroom conditions. I guess it's up to seven-year-olds to learn to cope with overcrowded classes and underpaid, overworked teachers. Remember being told as a child, "Actions speak louder than words"? It's time we pay attention to what our elected officials actually do, and ignore what they say.

I've never been a Democrat. I've never been a Republican. I got into local politics when I was twenty-one years old as a Green Party organizer. For the past seven years, I've worked with other people in my community to create a political party that will give people hope, that won't compromise or sell out our democracy, our environment, our health, and our pursuit of happiness.

I'm twenty-seven, the mayor of New Paltz, New York, and the second American mayor ever to perform gay marriages. I'm writing this book because there are problems in this country that the American people must solve, and we aren't given the tools we need to solve them. We aren't taught in high school or college how to run for office, plan a protest, or organize civil disobedience—basic ways to participate directly and meaningfully in our society.

I've been an activist for around ten years. I'm not an expert. I'm just someone who has been engaged in grassroots political action and spent a lot of my time trying to piece together what I've learned along the way. There are thousands of books that deal with the environment, equal rights, and the economy in more detail than I'm able to. I'm not a scholar. But as a housepainter (among other things) since the age of fifteen, I know a lot about working for a living to make the rent and pay the bills. More and more, I feel that time has run out, that something has to be done to improve our lives now, not later. There's no time to read every book on every issue. There's no time to wait for the "experts" to figure out the perfect solution to every problem. We need to take matters into our own hands, and we don't need to know every statistic about every issue to have an opinion and act on it.

I'm writing this book because change isn't just possible,

it's inevitable. And it's in our power, as a people, to change things for the better.

We can shape our communities into anything we want. We just need to know what we want, figure out who has the ability to give it to us, and then, if they're unwilling, figure out how to force them to. There are practical solutions to our energy and environmental crises, our civil rights failures, and our undemocratic election system. Change is inevitable. We might as well steer it in the direction we want, instead of letting it roll over us.

It's up to us to get what we want because politicians are only human. Corruption isn't the either/or that most people think. Some of the most well-meaning, sincere politicians become corrupted because they get burned out, their supporters lose interest in an issue after the first round is fought, they want to appease someone quickly, or they're tempted by power and wealth. Politicians are not, generally speaking, evil, but they're not perfect either. We simply can't expect elected officials to be and do everything we need. We have to look to ourselves to pick up the slack when a good politician falters or a bad one storms ahead.

Too many of us believe that we can't make a difference

in the world. We feel too average to affect people in obvious positions of power; we think people with wealth or political leverage won't listen to us. But they only have power over us if we give it to them. We have so much more leverage than we know.

There's no time left to turn away from the political process. Our global climate teeters on the edge of a cliff, and our national deficit, at 7.7 trillion dollars, is obscene. While our government spends billions fighting in Iraq every week, millions of American citizens at home go without medical care, a job, a free college education, or a decent meal. What do you want to fight for? What are you willing to do? Politics is about power. Who has it and who doesn't is literally a life-and-death issue. If your representatives are not doing what you want, you need to find a way to force them to.

To take responsibility for our lives, we need to understand how change happens. We need to understand the power we have. We need to put our hopes into action.

This book is for people who aren't happy with the way things are but don't know exactly why; or if they know why, they don't know what to do about it. I want to talk about tangible goals and tactical ways to achieve them. I don't have all the answers or a lifetime of experience, but I've been working on the ground for a good while trying to figure out how to be effective. I've got a few ideas and hopefully they'll be useful to others.

Activism is, after all, the oldest American tradition. The revolutionary patriots, the abolitionists, Henry David Thoreau, Harriet Tubman, Susan B. Anthony, the United Farm Workers, Dr. Martin Luther King, Jr. and all the millions of Americans whose names we'll never know who have marched, gone to jail, been blacklisted, or spoken up to protest inhumanity and injustice were activists.

Modern American society has painted activists and radicals as irrational, out-of-touch, dangerous people who would destroy the fabric of our peaceful lives. Or else we're told that activists' hearts are in the right place but their ideas simply aren't practical. Our Revolutionary ancestors were practical when they refused to pay taxes to England and dumped a shipload of tea into the ocean in protest: if they hadn't, the United States might still be a colony of the British Empire. Women who protested, marched, and were jailed until they won the right to vote were nothing if not levelheaded.

And every one of them was told he or she couldn't win.

The Revolutionaries were told that they could never fight the British Empire, the abolitionists were told that they could never defeat the slave power, women were told that they would never get the right to vote, Greens were told that they could never win office, and gays were told that they would never be able to marry. The only way to make sure you don't win is to not fight. The one way to make sure you lose is to give up.

I want to talk about why the current voting system must be changed and how to change it so that it represents the whole country, not just a privileged few. I want to talk about how we can make significant environmental improvements, without waiting for the president to solve everything at once. He won't—he's working against us— so let's you and I get started. I want to talk about human rights and what we can do to promote equality for all. And I want to talk about the myth of the market system and how we can weaken the corporate stranglehold on our lives. We need to take matters into our own hands and regain our dignity as a democracy. Everyone has some issues they're more concerned about than others. If you live in farm country, you're more concerned about agriculture and rural issues than you are gang violence. If you live in a city, you're more concerned with the failed war on drugs and the warehousing of blacks and Latinos in prisons. The issues I bring up are important to me because of where I grew up and where I live. They're obviously not the only things worth fighting for, but they are the issues I know the most about.

Finally, I want to talk about power. It all comes down to that. For people who are actively trying to change the world, the most important conversation we can have is about power—and about making activism a part of our lives in a way that's fun and sustainable, not just something you do in an emergency.

Some of us have an hour a week to offer, some an hour a day; some of us will feel compelled to make our political work full time. At whatever level, local or national, and with whatever time we can give, our participation is the first step to our getting power over our own lives. Writing a letter to your congressman is fine, but it won't give you enough of a voice to compete with campaign contributions. We need to find the right leverage points.

Change is constant, but it's rarely fast. Once in a while, decades of organizing will suddenly erupt into a huge, unstoppable social movement. More often, it's hard to tell if we're gaining ground or not. It can be hard to keep going, to organize another antiwar demonstration not knowing if anyone will listen and suspecting that few will. It can be even harder for young activists. Some family members used to tell me that being politically radical was just a phase, that I'd grow out of it. They weren't against it; they saw it as a normal adolescent detour from some straight path I'd eventually get back on. An uncle of mine used to say, "If you're not a liberal at twenty, you have no heart. If you're not a conservative at fifty, you have no brains." That's often the reaction to young activists by people who gave up their faith in their ability to change anything. It can be devastating to be told you'll "grow out of it" when you are fighting for something you believe in. I still remember meeting veteran organizers who had been fighting for civil rights and against war for thirty, forty, or fifty years. These were people who could have been my grandparents marching with me at protests or talking over a beer about what it was like to be an activist in the 1930s. Their example gave me strength and hope. Writing this book will have been worth it if just one teenager finds it and understands that having firm beliefs and acting on them need not be "just a phase" and that other people are out there who feel the way she does and have been fighting for their convictions their entire lives.

America is sick with corruption. We don't have to be. Political action should be a constant part of our lives. Let's teach our children by example to participate in democracy. We can't just be active when there's an emergency; that's like waiting until you have a heart attack to decide that you want to be healthy. Activism is preventive medicine; the more people who are politically active as part of their daily lives, the healthier our society will be.

ONE

We Hold These Truths

We hold these truths to be self-evident, that all men are created equal, that they are endowed by their Creator with certain unalienable Rights, that among these are Life, Liberty and the pursuit of Happiness . . .

Thomas Jefferson

My ancestors came to the Hudson Valley, where I live, in the 1650s, gambling they could make better lives for themselves living on the frontier with the Esopus Indians and the Dutch. Two hundred fifty years ago, my family went to war for life, liberty, and the pursuit of happiness. There were lots of reasons why people took up guns in the Revolution, but the moral compass of our Revolutionary writing still guides our sense of what it means to be an American. The Declaration of Independence is the founding and defining psalm of our country.

. . . that all men are created equal, that they are en-dowed by their Creator with certain unalienable Rights, that among these are Life, Liberty and the pursuit of Happiness.—That to secure these rights, Governments are instituted among Men, deriving their just powers from the consent of the governed . . .

In the centuries since, people's movements have called on the memory of the Revolution to define what's right and what's wrong. That Declaration was called upon to defend a woman's right to vote and the abolition of slavery—the creation of civil rights for those of us who didn't fall into the narrow class of property-owning white men that ended up running the country.

Democracy is a simple, powerful idea. Life, liberty, and the pursuit of happiness. It means people—all of us—have the right to an equal voice in the cooperative running of our society and government. It isn't democracy if only people who own property can vote. It isn't democracy if men can run for office, but women can't. It isn't democracy when blacks are lynched for voting or running for office. It isn't democracy if rich people can run for office but poor people can't. It isn't democracy if only two points of view are allowed to be heard.

We live in a country with almost 300 million people. Americans speak hundreds of languages, practice dozens of religions (mostly one at a time), and hold a range of passionate political opinions that a simple red state–blue state map can't begin to illustrate. We live in a country with obscene wealth and abject poverty, and the trust fund baby and the guy who works at McDonald's have an equal right to be heard. And if we had a democracy, both of them would have a shot at arguing their politics in the halls of Congress.

*   *   *

The firehouse was crowded on election night. Twenty minutes before the polls closed, local politicians outside were muttering to me "You won" and "Congratulations" as I walked in to witness the vote count. Running on a platform of environmental protection, open government, tenants' rights, and affordable housing, I had begun campaigning for mayor of New Paltz only six weeks before, on a slate with two other community organizers—Rebecca Rotzler and Julia Walsh, each running for village trustee.

When the results were announced, I thought they were being read in order, starting with the winner. Jean Gallucci, the clerk treasurer, read, "In the election for mayor, Tom Nyquist, two hundred fifty-one votes." My stomach clenched. Nodding to myself, I pasted a small smile on my lips, as defeat and depression opened their familiar, welcoming arms. There it was again, that background hum of despair and resignation, and the relentless plodding on to the next day. In an ancient Greek myth, Sisyphus is cursed to push a boulder up a hill, only to find that once he nears the top, the boulder always overwhelms him and rolls back down, forcing him to start all over again, for eternity. When I heard Tom's name read first, I placed my hands on the boulder to start pushing again, with the hope that next time things would be different, but I knew in my heart that our side would lose again. I also knew that we'd keep trying.

Jean read, "Robert Feldman, two hundred forty-nine." I felt exposed, sitting at a table on our side of the yellow-taped boundary line laid down to keep people away from the vote counting. The candidates and vote counters were on one side of the line, while reporters, spectators, friends and families stood on the other, pressed together shoulder to shoulder, jostling, sweaty, unable to move without stepping on someone else's foot or elbowing someone accidentally.

I was wrong about the order. "Jason West, three hundred twenty-two." The shock hit me and the crowd at the same time. Stunned, I heard screams in the distance and cheering. I heard my dad yell into his cell phone, "Your nephew's a mayor! Your nephew's a mayor!"

That night we swept the elections, unseating the man who had been mayor for sixteen years, as well as defeating his heir apparent. In the weeks after our election, the newspapers and our opponents would tell stories of how we had been elected by "the students," saying we had mobilized ignorant college kids to come out and vote in an election they had no business participating in. In this small town of six thousand people, 80% of us are under the age of forty. The old guard saw students as a nuisance, a transient population— even if many stay after they finish school and all of us are the backbone of the local economy. For the old guard, though, anyone under thirty was by definition a "student" and had no right to a voice in our community government.

The press that night washed over us like a tide. Four or five reporters and a camera were in my face taking down my reactions, while I sat dazed and grinning, my shoulders straighter, trying to sound mayoral.

*   *   *

The American election system, as it's run today, is undemocratic. There is something very wrong with elections that bully you into supporting someone you don't want to support. The pressure to follow the party line (Democrat or Republican) even if you don't like it—to vote against someone you hate rather than for someone you admire—caught everyone's attention in our last two presidential elections. The pressure to vote against your conscience shows up in local elections, too.

I ran for mayor as one of four candidates: two Democrats, an independent (who ran as a protest candidate and got thirty-four votes), and myself as the Green. The incumbent mayor, Tom Nyquist, was being challenged by his heir apparent, Robert Feldman. Tom had been mayor for sixteen years, with four years as deputy mayor before that. Robert had been on the village board for eight years. The story goes that Robert had already been campaigning for months when he and Tom had a falling out. Tom had been set to retire from public service but all of a sudden decided to run for another term. For a year before the elections, Tom and Robert argued with each other at village board meetings and publicly tried to draw a sharp line between themselves. People were taken aback, since the two men had previously run for office together, Tom for mayor and Robert for trustee.

Like most politicians, Tom and Robert spent little time explaining why they were a good candidate and most of their time explaining why their opponent was a bad one. My two running mates and I decided to campaign without publicly attacking or criticizing our opponents. We focused on explaining to people what we wanted to do in office. We explained our vision for the future of the community—the projects we wanted to work on, the laws we wanted to pass. We laid out specific things we'd do to bring affordable housing, smart growth, tenants' rights, a healthy environment, and more open government to our village. If you agree with our ideas, we said, please consider supporting us on election day.

Many people I spoke to said they liked what I had to say and wanted to vote for me but couldn't because they didn't think I could win. When I asked why they preferred Nyquist, most people said because he wasn't Feldman. And those who preferred Feldman did so, they told me, because he wasn't Nyquist. People weren't rude enough to come out and say it that way, of course. Instead, they said they wanted Robert because Tom had been mayor so long, it was time to get some new blood in office. Or they wanted Tom because they didn't think Robert would make a good mayor. No one I spoke to said they were voting for Nyquist because they liked what he stood for. No one said they were voting for Feldman because they agreed with his vision for the community.

In the week before the election, the local *Times-Herald Record* ran a half-page story on the candidates. Most of the article described the election as between Nyquist and Feldman; it described their past working relationship as that of mentor and protégé, then discussed their falling out. The only mention of my candidacy was at the very end of the article:

> Both [Nyquist and Feldman] are registed Democrats and are running on tickets that include well-known and popular figures. And both men are quick to discount the potential impact of Green Party candidate Jason West's candidacy.
>
> "In a small village election like this, anyone is free to run for office, whether they're qualified or not," Feldman said.
>
> For his part, Nyquist didn't see any echo of things past in running against a young, environmentally minded candidate with a presumably strong college-age constituency.
>
> "All the candidates were on campus recently, and as far as I could see, there were only about 20 students who showed up," Nyquist said.

To be fair, the *Record* ran other articles that did cover the issues we were raising in our campaign, as did the other dailies and the weekly *New Paltz Times*. But the article above makes an important point. Despite all our volunteers and campaign posters, despite all the energy and excitement we generated, a significant part of the community didn't think we could win and was therefore trapped into voting for someone else. Voting for our slate, in some parts of New Paltz, was seen as a waste of time. Even worse, some people wanted to vote for me but didn't because if they didn't vote for Feldman, Nyquist might get in, or the other way around.

There's no way to tell how many votes I would have gotten if more of our supporters had been convinced we could win. How many people who voted for Feldman only in fear of Nyquist might have voted for us? How many lukewarm supporters of Nyquist would have come to our ticket if they'd thought we had a chance? How many people stayed home who might have voted Green, except they read that article and figured we couldn't win?

You don't need support from the majority of voters to win an election, you just need to be able to get more votes than anyone else. At the end of the day, I won the mayor's race with 38 percent of the vote. Nyquist and Feldman spent a year fighting over the same base of five hundred voters and split them almost exactly down the middle.

But even the way we report elections is slanted.

While I got 38 percent of the vote, that means I got support from 38 percent of the people who voted, *not* 38 percent of the village residents. When you add in all the people who were registered to vote and didn't, and all the people who are eligible to vote but aren't registered, I won the mayoralty with the support of 6 percent of the adult population of the village. I won with 322 votes in a village of six thousand people.

Something is obviously wrong with our democracy if someone can get all the power with 6 percent of the people voting for him. And it's the same for every election. Next time you hear election returns, make sure you adjust the math. Look up your town or city on the census website and check out how many people live there who are over eighteen. That's the voting age population. Then keep that number in mind next time elections come around, and you'll be able to see exactly how little active support it takes to win an election.

But it doesn't have to be this way, and if we want a diverse democracy, it can't be this way.

The first thing we've got to do is get rid of the spoiler effect. No one should be forced to vote for someone she doesn't want in order to make sure someone worse doesn't get elected. Our winner-take-all elections work fine as long as there are only ever two points of view, two candidates to choose from, two parties to vote for, because the majority of people are going to choose one or the other. Or maybe, given two bad choices, most people will decide not to make a choice at all, and stay home.

In a country of 296 million people, though, we can't rely on the Democratic and Republican parties to bring to the floor of Congress the full spectrum of political opinion in our country. We can't expect two parties dedicated to the defense of corporate America to bring passionate arguments and policy to defend those of us who are not CEOs. We need a government as diverse as we are. We won't get one if we're constantly told that we can't vote for the candidate we respect, because they'll never win, and voting our conscience delivers victory into the hands of our least favorite candidate. Our voting system is fundamentally undemocratic. If our voting system is flawed, so is our democracy.

The simplest way to make sure there's no spoiler effect

is to run our elections using instant runoff voting (IRV). With IRV, instead of voting for one candidate and ignoring the rest, you rank the candidates in order of your preference. If there are four candidates, instead of voting for one, you mark each candidate one through four in order of how much you would like them to hold office. If one candidate gets a majority of the votes right off the bat, then that candidate wins. If no candidate gets a majority, then the person with the least amount of support is eliminated and all the people who voted for that person as their first choice have their vote go to their second choice. You keep eliminating candidates this way until someone has a majority. With IRV, whoever wins has at least some support of the majority of people; and there's no such thing as a spoiler effect, so the outcome of elections is more honest.

Instant runoff voting is already in use by the cities of Cambridge, Massachusetts, and San Francisco, California. It's used to elect officers of Democratic Party clubs in New York City and within the Utah Republican Party, along with half a dozen towns across the country. It's used all over the world to elect, for instance, the president of Ireland and the Australian senate.

Instant runoff voting is based on a few simple assumptions. The first is that anyone who holds public office needs to have the support of a majority of the voters. Many communities use traditional runoff elections: if no one wins a majority the first time around, there's another election a few weeks later with only the top two vote getters on the ballot. In our case, here in New Paltz, I was the top voter getter with 38 percent of the vote, but that's obviously not a majority. If local law said the mayor had to get the support of a majority of the voters, we would have been required to have a runoff election. Tom Nyquist, with 251 votes, came in second, so it would have been a runoff between Tom and me; everyone would have had to come back a few weeks after the initial election and choose between the two of us.

The problem is, runoff elections are expensive. Cost shouldn't matter when it comes to making sure that elections are fair, but faced with making elections fair and spending more money, too many politicians will go with the cheaper option rather than raise taxes. Runoff elections are also clumsier: it's hard enough to get people out to vote the first time around, without having to tell them they need to vote again a few weeks later, so voter turnout drops.

Instant runoff voting is a way to have all the benefits of traditional runoff voting without the downsides. With IRV, we know our public officials are elected by a majority of voters; there's no spoiler effect; more people run for office, so we get more than two choices to vote for—all with only one trip to the school gym or church basement!

The way it works is simple: instead of pulling the lever for one person, you rank your choices. In the 2003 mayoral election, I voted for myself. If we had had instant runoff voting, I might have voted:

1) Jason West
2) Tom Nyquist
3) Robert Feldman
4) Carl Heissenbuttel

Under our current system, I got more votes than anyone else, so I won. With instant runoff voting, getting more votes than anyone else isn't enough. You need to get support from a majority of the voters.

In our mayoral election, Carl got the fewest votes (34). With IRV, he would be eliminated, and the vote of everyone who put Carl as their first choice would then go to their second choice. Since everyone who voted for Carl for mayor also voted for the two women I was running with for village board, it's a safe bet Carl's votes would have gone to me. That brings me up to 42 percent of the vote. That's still not a majority.

After Carl, Robert got the fewest votes, so he would then be eliminated. The 249 people who voted for Robert would then have their votes go to their second choice. Since 856 people voted, and you need over 50 percent of those votes to get a majority, whoever gets 429 votes becomes mayor. With Carl out, this is where we'd stand:

Jason West	356 or 42% of the vote
Tom Nyquist	251 or 29% of the vote
Robert Feldman	249 or 29% of the vote

I'd need another 73 votes to get a majority and win; Tom would need another 178 votes.

There's no way to tell how many of Feldman's voters would have chosen Nyquist as their second choice and how many would have chosen me. But since I'm the one writing the book, and since for the most part I always liked Tom, let's say he and I split Feldman's votes down the middle, each of us getting 124. That puts the tally at

Jason West   480 votes or 56% of the vote
Tom Nyquist   375 votes or 44% of the vote

Even though the outcome of the election wouldn't change, it would be clear what direction the community wanted to go in. If in the example above Tom had gotten all of Robert's second-place votes and won the election instead of me, it would have been clear that the community wanted a different vision than the one Rebecca, Julia, and I offered. The power and elegance of IRV is that it makes absolutely clear what the voters want, by allowing us to vote our conscience without fear.

In 2004, millions of people voted for Kerry not because they liked Kerry but because they hated Bush. And then there were the millions of people four years previously who couldn't stand Bush but were afraid that if they voted for Pat Buchanan, Gore might win. If we take the fear out of voting, then wouldn't election returns be more honest? Wouldn't our elected officials more accurately represent we, the people? We would have more people running for office, because they'd stand a chance to win. More people would vote, because they'd know that if they voted outside the Democratic/Republican box, they wouldn't spoil the election for the more "viable" candidate. If people can vote for the person they truly want in office, more candidates are viable!

We've been overwhelmed the past few years by an "anyone but Bush" mentality. People think that Bush is so bad, we need to support whomever the Democrats put forward. What this line of thinking ignores is that Bush could not push his agenda without the help and support of the Democrats in Congress. All of Bush's appointments, for instance, need to be ratified by the Senate. The president nominates someone and puts his or her name forward. Any federal judge or cabinet member must be voted up or down by the Senate. John Ashcroft would not have been attorney general overseeing the systematic gutting of our Bill of Rights without the active support and complicity of the Senate Democrats. Gale Norton would not be secretary of the interior, reigning over environmental destruction, without the active help of the Senate Democrats.

In 2000 and 2004, the life-or-death issue was abortion. We in the Green Party were told by Democrats that we couldn't run someone for president because we'd take votes away from the Democratic nominee and spoil the election: Bush would get in and appoint tons of pro-life judges to the bench, especially the Supreme Court. What they ignored then and ignore now is that it is not the president who appoints justices, it is the Senate. The Senate bears responsibility for who gets approved. Antonin Scalia, for example, arguably the most pro-life justice on the Supreme Court, was appointed unanimously by the Senate in the 80s, when Al Gore was a senator from Tennessee and John Kerry was a senator from Massachusetts. Senators Gore and Kerry voted to put Scalia on the Supreme Court, ignoring the outcries of pro-choice women's health advocates around the country. Of the three major presidential candidates in the last two elections, it was Al Gore and John Kerry who had a proven track record of appointing a pro-life justice to the Supreme Court. It was Democrat Al Gore and Democrat John Kerry, not Republican George W. Bush, who undermined *Roe v. Wade* on the Supreme Court.

For radicals and for progressives (in other words, for people with common sense), to vote Democratic is to take part in an abusive relationship. There are people in the world who honestly believe that war is good, that poor people should pay more taxes than rich people, that our economy and foreign policy should be geared toward making sure that multinational corporations make huge profits. There are people who think it's a good idea that small businesses, workers, and the self-employed shoulder the burden to give tax breaks to the corporate sector. There are people who honestly believe that kids in poor neighborhoods deserve shitty schools and kids in rich neighborhoods deserve great schools. For those people, it makes sense to vote for Democrats and for Republicans; they can choose which candidate to vote for based on charisma or style or haircut, safe in the knowledge that in every important policy decision, they will get what they want regardless. The rulers of our country have in place a very well-oiled game of good cop–bad cop. We are told that the only answer to the neofascism of Bush and the Republicans is to support the Democrats. Fear, apathy, and laziness make that a very appealing option. Instead of doing the hard daily work of forging America into the democracy we all want, it's so much easier to just pull the lever for a Democrat, simply because he's not a Republican.

So it isn't just empty talk when people say the Democrats and Republicans are alike. If you go by the record and not the rhetoric, the Democrats don't look much different from their Republican colleagues. With neither party looking out for what's good for the American people, we desperately need more parties able and willing to fill that void.

*   *   *

The day after we won election, all I wanted to do was rest. We had been out in public as much as possible for six weeks, knocking on doors, speaking to community groups, sitting in endless meetings, and talking to the press. I thought now we would have some time off to recuperate. I thought our victory would get us an article in the *New Paltz Times* and a back page story in the three dailies that cover New Paltz. By midmorning my answering machine was full (and would keep filling up every few hours for three days). We were front page news in the *Kingston Freeman* four out of the next seven days; congratulatory calls were coming from California, e-mails from Greens in Texas, Ontario, and North Carolina. People were excited about our victory—Rebecca and I as Greens, Julia as an Independent—because it had seemed impossible.

What we did was give people hope. No one believed that our side could win, the odds were stacked too high against us. The obstacles to winning were overwhelming. In the weeks after our election, people would come up to me—people I had never met and people I've known for years—and say, "You've given me so much hope." What they saw was that it *is* possible to win without compromising your principles. It is possible to break out of the deadly cycle of fear and despair that entraps us when we always choose the lesser of two evils, knowing that every time you choose the lesser of two evils, you get evil. Hope is the first step toward making change. People have to understand that it's possible to shape the world we want.

The odds are so against us that most people can't face down the struggle for freedom over fear, for justice over greed. We don't want to rock the boat; we want security, even at the cost of freedom. We choose to ignore common sense and do what we are told. When told, via the Patriot Act, that we need to give up our civil rights in order to protect our freedom, every true American should recoil in horror, feel a clenching in their gut, and trust their instincts that America itself is being drowned in the bathtub down the hall. Instead, we cling to whatever comforts we have—our house or job or clients or car or TV—and we obey. Our minds have been very carefully guided by our government, with its color-coded alerts and talk of shooting down terrorists John Wayne–style till every last one is killed. Is this the America we want?

For most of us, for the backbone of America, for small business owners, for the self-employed, for wage workers and college students, we need something different from the fearmongering that our government passes off as policy. We see the need for America to live up to its self-image as a beacon of democracy in the world, a haven of peace and freedom, a refuge from political or religious persecution.

We need to be able to debate those who disagree with us on equal footing—in state legislatures, in town halls, and on the floor of Congress.

If we're going to have real, full democracy, if we're going to have thorough debate and arguments decide the direction of our country, we the people need our own political parties. We need to change the rules of the game to allow more voices to be heard. We need full, mandatory public financing of elections. We need presidential debates that include all of the candidates for president, not just two. Let's let them all up on stage and let the voters decide who makes sense. Let the voters decide who deserves to be president, not the corporate-owned media. We can't let the corporate news networks tell us that only two presidential candidates deserve to be heard, and we must choose between them, even though there are dozens of presidential candidates on the ballot. Let the American people decide if the Green Party candidate, the Libertarian, or the Natural Law candidate will lead this country in the direction they want it to go. Let the candidates defend themselves and the American people judge who is fit to govern.

In Democratic communities, Republicans have begun to join forces with Greens and Libertarians to support fair elections. In Alaska, for example, a ballot referendum to elect all federal offices using IRV was supported by the Greens and Republicans and fought bitterly by the Democratic Party. In heavily Republican communities, it's the Democrats who support IRV. We barely have even a two-party system in America. Instead we have competing archipelagos of a one-party system, designed on purpose to make sure that in County X you don't win office unless you're a Democrat and in County Y you don't win unless you're a Republican.

Every ten years, after the census, legislatures all over the country get together to choose who will vote for them. They draw congressional, state, and county legislature districts to make sure they know the outcome of an election before any votes are cast.

In 1812, Massachusetts governor Elbridge Gerry wanted to make sure that his political allies got elected. Figuring they would lose if there were a fair election, Gerry made sure to draw the district lines so that his allies couldn't lose. The best one he came up with was a salamander-shaped district, giving us the word *gerrymander* to describe a hideously contorted district obviously drawn for partisan reasons. In some cases, gerrymandering is useful. To make sure that communities don't end up with all-white legislatures, for example, we need to make sure some districts are drawn to elect African American, Hispanic, Asian, or Native American politicians.

These days politicians have the means to accurately predict every election. Today the element of chance has all but disappeared in legislative elections, and with it voter power. Census data today is so sophisticated that politicians know who votes Democrat and who votes Republican down to the last house on every street of every block in town. The party in control of the state legislature uses this data to carve out districts that will keep it in power. Whichever party controls the legislature makes sure it gets most of the seats, regardless of how many votes that party gets. Here in Ulster County, New York, Republicans and Democrats have been getting almost the same number of votes for years. It varies, depending on the year, but only by a few percentage points. But even though Democrats got nearly as many votes as Republicans countywide, our county legislature has almost always had a Republican supermajority. The Republicans simply make sure that most county legislative districts combine one Democratic community with two Republican communities, nearly guaranteeing a Republican win every time. It was only in the past two years, when Greens, Independents, "good government" groups, and an alert local press educated the Democrats and worked with a handful of firebrand Democratic allies, that activists here were able to force the Republicans to pass a better districting scheme.

Getting rid of gerrymandered districts, eliminating the need for affirmative action gerrymandering, and electing legislatures that more fully represent the will of the people are possible through something called proportional representation (PR). The thinking behind PR is fairly straightforward: parties should have support in legislatures in direct proportion to their support from the voters. If a party gets 10 percent of the vote, it should have 10 percent of the seats in government. Proportional representation is used by most other industrial democracies in the world: Germany, Israel, Sweden, New Zealand, Spain, Italy, and Finland use this system to elect their parliaments, to name a few. A few years ago New Zealand changed its election system from the one we use in the United States to proportional representation. They made the switch because a nonpartisan commission declared that proportional representation was more just and democratic than the winner-take-all system we use here.

There are dozens of ways to design elections to have the results match the diversity of opinion in the country. The International Institute for Democracy and Electoral Assistance, based in Sweden, has several handbooks on electoral system design on their website. Their guides are used by new democracies in the process of designing their constitutions and election systems. The simplest form is something called a party list system. For simplicity's sake, let's say we have a legislature of one hundred people. Since there are one hundred seats to fill, each party puts up a list of one hundred candidates, with their favorite or most popular names at the top of the list. On election day, we all pull the lever for the party that best represents us. Say the parties are the Democratic Party, Green Party, Republican Party, Black Panther Party, Reform Party, and American Nazi Party. When the votes are counted, say the Democratic Party gets 40 percent of the vote; the Green Party gets 7 percent; the Republicans get 43 percent; the Reform Party gets 1 percent; the Black Panther Party gets 8 percent; and the American Nazi Party gets 1 percent.

Since every party gets seats in the legislature in direct proportion to its support among the voters, then the Democratic Party would get 40 percent of the seats. In a one hundred person legislature, that means forty seats.

So, in the above scenario, our imaginary legislature would be made up of forty Democrats, seven Greens, forty-three Republicans, one Reformer, eight Black Panthers, and one Nazi. The legislature would exactly mimic the full spectrum of diversity of political opinion of the voters.

Although many major nonpartisan institutions have endorsed IRV and PR, many Republicans and Democrats are fighting against it. That's because they stand to lose power. They stand to lose votes in a system where people have real choices.

In countries that use instant runoff voting and proportional representation, voting participation has increased dramatically. When people can vote honestly, and their vote means something, they *want* to vote. All IRV and PR do is ensure a more accurate election result. Instant runoff voting and proportional representation simply record the will of the people, whichever way it leans.

In this country most elections are decided before we ever get to the voting booth. And once you're in office, you're in for life. The American Congress has a 98 percent incumbency rate. You have to wait for members to die or retire if you want them out.

It's finally possible to have a serious conversation about basic democratic reforms, because Americans have woken up to the problem of voting in our country. For the past two presidential elections the American people have been faced with some of the worst corruption (among Republicans) and most abject capitulation (among Democrats) in a very long time. Four years ago, for the first time in living memory, a president gained the office who lost the popular vote.

The Democratic Leadership Council—founded by Bill Clinton and others to pull the Democratic Party to the right—commissioned a study of the 2000 election by pollster Mark Penn. The DLC devoted the entire January 2001 issue of their bimonthly magazine, *Blueprint*, to the question, "Why Gore Lost and How the Democrats Can

Come Back." Al From, CEO of the DLC, argued that Gore lost the 2000 election because he chose to ignore the New Democrat strategy of focusing on the needs of affluent white men. Women, minorities, and people making less than $50,000 a year, he wrote, make up a shrinking percentage of the electorate. Democratic campaigns were advised to cater to their new electorate of wealthy, white, suburban men, not to people who used to vote but no longer see any reason to. In short, Al From and the DLC blamed Gore's loss of the presidency on his failure to be more conservative.

For those of us who voted for Nader, even as the Democrats crucified him as a spoiler, it was interesting to hear From himself say, "The assertion that Nader's marginal vote hurt Gore is not borne out by polling data. When exit pollers asked voters how they would have voted in a two-way race, Bush actually won by a point. That was better than he did with Nader in the race." In other words, according to the study commissioned by the DLC, Nader's presence in the race actually *helped* Gore, making it a closer race than it would otherwise have been.

Investigative reporter Greg Palast, who covered the 2000 election for the BBC, had another explanation for

Gore's loss that wasn't reported in the American press. Palast had uncovered a string of criminal actions by Florida governor Jeb Bush—brother of George W.—and Secretary of State Katherine Harris. Jeb Bush and Katherine Harris had methodically purged up to 90,000 voters from the Florida voter rolls. The overwhelming majority of the outlawed voters were black, and they were overwhelmingly from Democratic neighborhoods. In a January 26, 2005, column for the *Seattle Post-Intelligencer*, Palast said, "A U.S. Civil Rights Commission investigation concluded that, of nearly 180,000 votes discarded in Florida in the 2000 election as unreadable, a shocking 54 percent were cast by black voters, though they make up only a tenth of the electorate. In Florida, an African American is 900 percent more likely to have his or her vote invalidated than a white voter." We never heard about the Civil Rights Commission report on the nightly news in this country, though the BBC covered it exhaustively.

Presented with evidence of flagrant voter fraud in the 2000 election, the Congressional Black Caucus tried in 2001 to challenge the official certification of Bush's "election." With Vice President Al Gore presiding, not a single

U.S. senator—Democrat or Republican—agreed to join with the members of the Congressional Black Caucus. Most Americans didn't learn about that particular failure of the Senate until they saw Michael Moore's *Fahrenheit 9/11*, and most who did were horrified by that missed opportunity for justice—or, at the very least, debate.

Palast would later discover that the racist purging of the Florida voting rolls continued unchecked into the 2004 presidential race. He found overwhelming evidence that the Republican Party engaged in a systematic targeting of black and Hispanic voters all over the country, challenging their right to vote and forcing them to vote on provisional ballots it made sure weren't counted.

Then there's the obvious: Gore lost the presidency because he gave up. Gore made his concession speech before the Florida recount was finished.

In the end, of the millions of votes cast across the country, only nine votes were counted. In a 5–4 decision, the Supreme Court appointed George W. Bush the president of the United States, calling a halt to the Florida recount while Bush was ahead but before all the ballots were counted.

Of all the issues surrounding the 2000 election, the

one perhaps most widely reported and discussed was the Electoral College. Most of us thought we were voting for the president, only to find out that all these years we were voting for electors, and that the electors, not the people, voted for the president.

The most common (and often only) argument heard in favor of the Electoral College is that the Founding Fathers wrote it into the Constitution to give small states some power over national affairs. The story goes that small states like Delaware and New Jersey were afraid that more populated states like New York or Virginia would always decide the presidency and that the interests of small states would be pushed aside in favor of the interests of more heavily populated states. That same argument has been used over the past five years to justify keeping the Electoral College, and to keep any discussion of abolishing it off the floor of Congress.

The reality of the Electoral College is more interesting, and would be more controversial were it ever discussed.

The Electoral College was not, as popular myth would have it, the finely crafted institution of brilliant men. At the Constitutional Convention, the Electoral College was a rush compromise added at the end of a long, hot summer, when the delegates were tired. It was voted on with little discussion and less debate.

Then, as now, the divisions in the country had little to do with population density: you don't see New York and Texas ganging up on Rhode Island, or California and Ohio teaming up against Wyoming. Until the late twentieth century, the country was divided along sectional lines, North versus South. We forget that when the Electoral College was created, slaves, women, Native Americans, and white men without property couldn't vote. The number of electors each state had was based on the number of people in that state, not the number of voters, with slaves counted as only three-fifths of a person. The point was not how many people were in each state but how many rich white men were in each state.

The northern states had more property-owning white men than the southern states did. If the presidency were decided by the number of voters who could actually cast ballots, the North would dominate the presidency and likely move to abolish slavery. The South's answer was to base presidential elections on how many people—not voters—were in each state. The slaves in Virginia would give the white voters in that state more power. In fact, the

more slaves there were, and the fewer white property owners, the more power was concentrated in the hands of the
plantation owners. For the South, the system worked per-
fectly, resulting in the election of a slave-owning Virginian
to the presidency for thirty-two of the first thirty-six years
of the office.

Because representation in Congress and the Electoral
College is based on population, for two hundred years
the South has had power in Washington out of proportion to its number of voters. Even after Emancipation,
the South benefited from the racial politics of the Constitution. After the Civil War, while technically blacks
could vote, the elaborate Jim Crow laws made it realisti-
cally nearly impossible. Since most black Americans lived
in the South, their presence combined with their disen-
franchisement meant more representation and power for
white Southerners.

The undemocratic nature of the Electoral College has
been recognized since the beginning of the Republic. The
proof is that the Electoral College has been the target of
more attempts at reform than any other institution—
nearly a thousand proposed amendments, according to

the Center for Voting and Democracy—and all of them have failed.

In 1969, though, the Electoral College came close to being eliminated. In the previous year's presidential election, segregationist George Wallace gained forty-six electoral votes, sparking fears that neither Richard Nixon nor Hubert Humphrey would get enough electoral votes to win and Wallace would decide the presidency by giving his electoral votes to one of them. As it turned out, Nixon got a landslide. But the mere possibility that a third-party candidate could get enough votes to become kingmaker scared Congress into action on voting reform. A resolution for direct election of the president (with a runoff if no one got more than 40 percent of the vote) was wildly popular in the House, passing 338–70. When President Nixon publicly announced he would sign the bill once the Senate approved it, direct election of the president seemed a reality.

That reality was destroyed by the racial politics of the South. The bill to eliminate the Electoral College never even came up for a vote. When it was filibustered by racist senators like James Eastland of Mississippi and

Strom Thurmond of North Carolina, there were two separate votes to shut down debate—known as a vote for cloture—and bring the bill to a vote. Both attempts to stop the filibuster failed, and the bill to eliminate the Electoral College was dead, put off indefinitely.

The cloture votes were critical. We can assume that those who voted for cloture—to end discussion and vote on the measure—were in favor of direct election of the president and that those who voted not to end cloture were opposed. Over two-thirds of Senate Democrats and one-half of Senate Republicans favored ending debate and voting on eliminating the Electoral College. The senators from the twenty-six smallest states were evenly divided. If the Electoral College protected the interests of small states, it's fair to assume that senators from *all* those states would have voted to keep it.

Of the southern senators, only six voted to end debate and vote for direct election of the president, while twenty voted against. Of all the votes against direct election, 60 percent came from the South.

If racially biased purges of election rolls and use of

provisional ballots are any evidence, Jim Crow and racial politics are still very much alive. In the interest of "stability" and "moving on," the calls for justice by the Congressional Black Caucus in 2001 were ignored by the Senate which didn't have a single black member. In 2004, when Ohio and New Mexico's electoral votes went to Bush, there were more provisional ballots "thrown out" than the difference between Bush and Kerry: in Ohio, for example, Bush officially led by 136,000, but there were over 155,000 people whose votes were never counted. These uncounted votes came overwhelmingly from poor and black precincts, and according to the BBC, they were deliberately targeted by Kenneth Blackwell, Ohio's secretary of state and co-chair of the Bush-Cheney campaign.

The Electoral College, in short and without a doubt, facilitates racism. The most common argument against the Electoral College is that it's "outdated," as if there used to be a good reason for it. But the idea of small-state vulnerability—the only "good reason" ever given—is nonsense and always was: what national interest would Vermont have that New York doesn't? States' rights were never the issue. For two hundred years, the expression "states' rights" has been code for "white supremacy." That was clear when George Wallace stood in the doorway of the University of Alabama in 1963, blocking integration. It was clear when Strom Thurmond and James Eastland won their fight to preserve the Electoral College in 1969.

We have a real chance now—with voter dissatisfaction at an all-time high—to abolish this "peculiar institution" and elect our president directly with IRV, so we'd have a White House occupied by someone who represents the will of the people.

*   *   *

The last bastions of democracy left in America are local elections. We won in New Paltz because our village has just six thousand residents. With just a few thousand potential voters, you can run a grassroots campaign and win. In small elections like ours, there are no expensive media campaigns, no paid consultants, no focus groups or polls. You knock on doors, you talk to people, you meet with local organizations and discuss whether you support their issues and what the possibilities are to work together. You go to the candidates' forum run by the local League of Women Voters or Chamber of Commerce. You talk to the local newspapers. In an election like ours, where only about nine hundred people voted, you could physically speak to every potential voter and explain why you want to hold office. Our campaign raised just over two thousand dollars—most of it in tens and twenties at fund-raisers held at local bars and restaurants or by people handing us five dollars on the street. We printed up a few thousand fliers and did one mailing. We had posters in the windows of local businesses. On this level, at this small scale, money plays no part because you need so little of it. Polling and focus groups and media presence have no part: people aren't voting because of your image, they're voting because they know you personally and trust you to do a good job.

And it's here at the local level that we're going to forge a democratic America. Because local politicians can win office without a lot of money, we can pass campaign finance reform without being punished by lobbyists and big campaign contributors. Local governments are in a position to show their residents that mandatory public financing of elections works. It would only cost a few thousand dollars to fully fund all the candidates for a village or town election.

At the local level, we have a better chance of passing IRV legislation to eliminate the spoiler effect in elections like mine. At the local level we can work to increase voter turnout. Some communities (such as villages in New York State) run their own elections and can decide when Election Day is. There is discussion in New Paltz about changing Election Day from a Tuesday to a weekend: the polls would open at nine a.m. on a Saturday morning and close at nine p.m. on Sunday night, giving people much more time to vote than only a few hours before or after work in the middle of the week.

At the local level, we can work to create a binding "none of the above" option in all elections. If NOTA wins, then you need to have a new election a few months later with all new candidates, and no one who lost to NOTA is allowed to be on the ballot.

*   *   *

Too often the only people who feel well represented by politicians are the wealthy executives who own them. Politicians are a business investment. When special interests and corporations dump huge amounts of money into a candidate's campaign, that candidate is not a free agent. He belongs to the corporations who bought him. Corporate executives understood this a century ago: buy a politician and he'll bring a good return on the investment.

By owning politicians, CEOs control the regulation and deregulation of their business. General Electric dumped PCBs in the Hudson River for thirty years, never bothering to test whether or not they were dangerous and ignoring suspected health concerns. Federal and state environmental agencies barely lifted a finger to stop them, in part because of the efforts of Republican Congressman Gerald Solomon and his successor John Sweeney, each widely known as the "Congressmen from GE."

Corporations are not in business to be nice or socially responsible. A few end up that way, either by legal force or because an ethical CEO decides that contributing something valuable to society counts too. But those CEOs are extremely rare. More commonly, the most brutally ambitious, materialistic people are the ones promoted to run a corporation—the people who are literally willing to do anything for money, because that's the bottom line at the office and in their life. They get richly rewarded, financially and socially, for being ruthlessly materialistic. Brutally ambitious, materialistic people don't generally become teachers, social workers, scientists, nurses, doctors, carpenters, or artists. They find the quickest road to a hefty bank account: corporate life. Corporate executives are in business to create need, sell product, and make money. With corporations at the nation's helm, profit making has become our national creed. Life, liberty, and the pursuit of happiness have been defined for the country as the right to make as much money as we can. Greed is too often America's driving force. These brutally ambitious and materialistic people with no or little interest in social values are running our country.

Corporate interests continually shove people's interests aside. In poll after poll, for example, most Americans—as many as 80 percent—want a system of universal health care. You walk into the doctor's office of your choice and you get the medical treatment you need and the government picks up the tab. It's a basic human right that we should all collectively pay for, like we pay for the military, schools, prisons, and hospitals. Yet even though 80 percent of Americans want it, there is no movement in Congress to give us what we want.

In 2000, while running as a Green Party candidate for state assembly, I spoke at a forum sponsored by Citizens for Universal Healthcare. The group of mostly senior citizens had asked Dr. Deborah Richter to speak. Dr. Richter, a physician, spent forty-five minutes explaining that free universal health care for everybody would be cheaper than our current system. She explained that America spends more money on HMO coverage for some people than it would cost to give free health care to everybody. I don't have health insurance, and friends of mine have gotten sick and been unable to get the care they needed because they lacked insurance or had inadequate coverage. I got up and spoke that day about my friend Jamie, who needed to have a medical procedure done quickly or risked death or the loss of half his face. He was shunted for weeks from one HMO to another while they avoided giving him the care he needed. His procedure was expensive, so his HMO didn't want to give it to him: it cut into their bottom line. I told Citizens for Universal Healthcare I thought that free universal health care is desperately needed in this country; it's a life-or-death issue for too many of my friends and family.

Also at that forum was Democratic U.S. representative Maurice Hinchey. Hinchey is billed as one of the most progressive congressmen in Washington. Hinchey told that audience that he agreed with Dr. Richter, that we need universal health care, that he personally already had it, as did every member of Congress as one of the perks of the job.

Then he said, "but that's just not where the conversation is at in Washington right now." Think about that. A progressive Democrat, telling his supporters to their face that he has to postpone their issue, even though their solution is cheaper, more effective, more efficient, and desperately needed or people die. That's not where the conversation's at in Washington, and our representative to Congress refused to start that conversation. Personally, I thought that's what we send people to Washington to do: start conversations and fight like hell for things important to the people they represent. I've spoken to Hinchey's staff about his comments and they've explained that with Republicans in control of the Congress, the Democrats are paralyzed, unable to pass vital legislation such as for an effective, universal health care system. But Maurice Hinchey has been in Congress since the early 1990's, when the Democrats controlled the White House, the Senate, and the House of Representatives. Even with all three branches of government under their control, the Democrats were unwilling to pass single payer health care legislation. One bill—HR1200—never even got out of committee. To Hinchey's credit, he has co-sponsored a series of bills to create a system of universal health care, but apparently even with his party in power, the conversation just wasn't there in Washington.

*　*　*

The movement for IRV and PR in the United States is gaining momentum. The Center for Voting and Democracy is educating people about these voting methods across the country. Senator John McCain and Governor Howard Dean support IRV. An Illinois poll showed majority support for IRV in presidential elections. In a Vermont referendum, forty-nine of fifty-one townships overwhelmingly supported it. In Alaska, a referendum was narrowly defeated that would have instituted IRV for all federal elections. And San Francisco is the first major city to adopt instant runoff voting for all their citywide elections, including for mayor.

Instant runoff voting and proportional representation are about power—pure and simple. The idea of taking power scares a lot of people, mostly middle-class liberals and progressives. Power is part of human relations, whether we like it or not. We can't wish it away. Many see power as inherently cruel and abusive, but power is neutral: it's a tool that can be dangerous or beneficial, depending on how it's used. We can take power and use it for our common good, or we can relinquish it, because we find it distasteful—then kick and scream when others take it and abuse us with it.

We need to take power, to take back our government at the grassroots, local level. We need people in power who are innovative, pragmatic, and principled. We can't wait to have democracy in America. If we let corporations run our government and our economy, our lives will get worse. It's as simple as that.

There's a serious misunderstanding about why people don't vote. The assumption is that people don't vote because they're stupid, ignorant, lazy, or apathetic. What if instead they're just really smart and don't want to vote for any of the candidates the corporate news and CEOs have told them to choose from? What if they don't like their choices and have been told over and over that unless they vote Democratic or Republican, they're wasting their time? They don't want to waste their time, so they don't vote.

Democracy for most people means voting, but what does voting mean in America? It means watching the news and letting the news corporations tell you who is a viable candidate. Viable means electable, which means, more or less, whoever has the most money and the best image.

But democracy means more than voting. Democracy isn't just the trip to the polls, it's living as cooperatively as we can, not simply taking everything we can for ourselves and screw everyone else. It's not about just being an individual, it's about being an individual in a community.

Democracy is taking the moral lessons we all learned from Mom and Mr. Rogers and applying them to real people in the real world as grown-ups. Treat others the way you want to be treated. If you don't have anything nice to say, don't say anything at all. Be honest. Don't lie. Don't cheat. Don't steal. Killing is bad. Don't put poison on our food or in our air or in our water. Don't take advantage of other people.

Our whole economy and culture, though, is based on stealing and taking advantage of others, on being cruel because cruelty means a higher profit margin. It's based on killing: think of all the corporate environmental negligence and corporate sponsorship of war that have led to human disease and death. Cruelty of the worst kind means a bigger bonus for executives. The business of America is business, because, we're told, we need to run our government like we run a company. Government is *not* a business and shouldn't be. Businesses, with a few exceptions, treat their workers badly if it will make them more money. Businesses, more often than not, lie and manipulate their customers if it will get them more money. Those businesses that are most successful—the

Fortune 500, the ones traded on NASDAQ and the Dow Jones—are those that break unions, send jobs to developing countries where they can be done on the cheap and in miserable conditions, and buy off government regulators. Nike sneakers are made by women in China and Vietnam because it's illegal to form independent unions there and therefore harder for workers to find the power, self-confidence, or strength to fight against armed guards and the threat of starvation.

Folksinger Utah Phillips once spoke at a Young Writers' Conference, where he was going to be followed by someone from the local Chamber of Commerce. Looking out over the crowd of young people, he said, "You're about to be told one more time that you're America's most valuable natural resource. Have you seen what they do to valuable natural resources? Have you seen a strip mine? Have you seen a clear-cut in a forest? . . . Don't ever let them call you a valuable natural resource! They're gonna strip-mine your soul! They're gonna clear-cut your best thoughts for the sake of profit . . ." As he was carried to the door, he yelled over his shoulder, "Make a break for it, kids!"

I don't want my government run like a business. I want

it run like the cooperative, community-based institution it's supposed to be. How about this radical idea: how about instead of voting for something evil, we all vote for something good? Can't find anything good worth voting for? Then it's your moral obligation to build it yourself. That's what we're doing with the Green Party. If you agree with the Green Party's ideas, join us. If you can't find a party whose convictions match yours, start building your own party.

In the face of a crumbling, corrupt democracy, communities across the nation are inventing solutions. The Uruguayan writer Eduardo Galeano once wrote, "Utopia is on the horizon. When I walk two steps, it takes two steps back. I walk ten steps and it is ten steps further away. What is utopia for? It is for this, for walking." Our government is shot through with people who have sold out whatever principles they once had in order to win power for themselves. And our country is full of people who don't lift a finger to change things because the change needed is so thorough and overwhelming that it seems impossible. Unless we can change everything overnight, they think, why should we even try?

There is another way. We can win concrete, substantial victories without compromising our principles. And we can make fundamental, sweeping change if we take the long view, seeing our small victories as steps toward the larger goal.

Two

In a Time of Moral Crisis

The hottest places in hell are reserved for those who, in a time of moral crisis, do nothing.

Dante

We asked the couples to be at Village Hall by ten A.M. Crowded into a small conference room on the second floor, they stood with their families, while key organizers, various lawyers, and I went over what might happen at noon and why we were convinced the marriages I would perform were legal, when the governor and the Department of Health said otherwise. We were subdued and formal with each other; occasionally we'd let out a nervous laugh. Halfway through our meeting, a couple walked in with their seven-year-old daughter, Rebecca, who stole our attention as the only one there dressed for a traditional wedding. Wearing a frilly white flower girl's dress and carrying a small basket of rose petals, Rebecca was a reminder that this day was not, in the end, about politics.

Though it was late February, the sky was a clear blue, the air was warm, and the sun shone down on the five hundred people who had come to bear witness. I walked out of Village Hall into an emotional sea. Everyone was overwhelmed by a sense of living in the moment. Words like "joy" can't begin to describe how it felt to be amid hundreds gathered together to watch people shrug off the clinging shroud of repression and claim their freedom.

Michael Zierler and Deputy Mayor Rebecca Rotzler gently and efficiently took the couples' names, let them know their place in order, and escorted them through the crowd of strangers and the dozens of reporters who had shown up on less than a day's notice to cover the weddings. I made the ceremonies short to get as many done as I could before being stopped by the police, who stood in a ring at the back of the crowd. After the first couple headed off smiling and the crowd cheered, I waited anxiously for the second to come up. After the third, my lawyer said, "They're not going to stop you. Go for it." By the end of the afternoon, twenty-five same-sex couples were legally married.

In the three days surrounding the marriages, New Paltz had eighteen hundred hits on its website, more than the previous two years together. We had invited press to come and spread the word that our community stood in solidarity with others in support of civil rights, but we never imagined the word would get beyond the borders of upstate New York. A few articles in nearby Poughkeepsie and Kingston, and maybe, if we got lucky, a back page in the *New York Times* were all we expected. We'd sent out a press release the day before to the local news outlets and, as a formality, the Associated Press. As soon as our news hit the wire services, we were, to our shock, inundated with phone calls, and satellite trucks began making the drive up from New York City.

On Friday, local organizers rounded up a team of volunteers to help with the crushing pace of phone calls, media requests, and visits. In less than twenty-four hours, New Paltz would not only host twenty-five same-sex weddings but also receive overwhelming attention from national and international press that would take weeks to dissipate. This would not be the festive but fairly quiet event we'd anticipated.

The lion's share of the work to pull it off was done by villagers whose names didn't get in the papers, while I got most of the attention and credit. I would try to use that attention to say why marriage equality is important; why civil unions aren't enough; that yes, I'm straight; and that marriage equality, while most directly benefiting gays and lesbians, is an issue of basic civil and human rights that every one of us needs to ensure are respected.

*   *   *

It started six months earlier when, just after getting elected, I asked our village attorney, Spencer McLaughlin, to look into the possibility of my performing gay marriages. He brought me a thick file of case law and citations, all of which boiled down to the fact that New York law neither banned nor explicitly condoned same-sex marriage.

New York State's Domestic Relations Law defines

marriage not as the union of one man and one woman, but as a contract between parties:

> *Marriage, so far as its validity in law is concerned, continues to be a civil contract, to which the consent of parties capable in law of making a contract is essential.*
> Article 3, Section 10,
> NYS Domestic Relations Law

This is the defining statute, the definition of a marriage according to New York State law. In New York, a marriage is a civil contract between consenting parties, not a union of one man and one woman.

The New York State Legislature, in fact, went out of its way to define what types of marriages would be illegal in New York. Incestuous marriages, such as those between mother and son, uncle and niece, or brother and sister, are illegal. Also voidable are marriages where one person involved is under eighteen, is incapable of giving consent due to a lack of understanding, is forced into it, or has been incurably mentally ill for at least five years. Nowhere on the list of illegal marriages are same-sex couples mentioned.

The legislature didn't outlaw same-sex marriage when it outlawed other forms of marriage. The legislature also avoided any mention of gender in its definition of marriage. It seems clear then that, intentionally or not, New York State law, as it stands, allows for same-sex marriage. Without changing a single law in Albany, same-sex couples already have full marriage equality. In fact, our state constitution requires it. New York's constitution, like that in many other states, requires equal protection under the law for all New Yorkers, regardless of gender. When I was elected, I took an oath of office to defend that constitution.

The Department of Health, however, took it upon itself to violate our state constitution and illegally discriminate against gay and lesbian couples. The Department of Health is the agency that issues marriage licenses.

Over the past year, the DOH had sent a memo to all town and city clerks instructing them not to issue licenses to gays and lesbians or risk facing criminal charges. I don't know why the memo was sent. Maybe after a few other states allowed or discussed allowing same-sex marriage, some conservatives in Albany thought the memo would prevent an epidemic of tolerance. The DOH reasoned that since their marriage license form had a space for the groom's name and a space for the bride's name, same-sex partners couldn't fill it out. If they couldn't fill out the form, then they couldn't get married. Despite the fact that our constitution requires equal protection under the law, despite the fact that the law defines marriage as a contract between parties, not as the union of a bride and groom, the DOH decided that a form one of its own bureaucrats had created would rule as law, and marriage would therefore only be allowed between a man and a woman.

Following my conscience and upholding my oath of office, I refused to go along with Department of Health policy. Our town clerk refused to issue licenses to same-sex couples, preferring to obey the Department of Health. Thankfully, New York law doesn't require a license for a couple to be legally married; all it requires, according to Article 3, Section 25, is for the ceremony to be properly solemnized:

Nothing in this article contained shall be construed to render void by reason of a failure to procure a marriage license any marriage solemnized between persons of full age.

Even if you don't have a marriage license, then, your marriage is legal as long as it's solemnized. "Solemnization" happens when the proper authority—a mayor, cleric, or judge—announces the couple married, saying, "By the power vested in me by the State of New York, I now pronounce you . . ." The final words—"husband and wife," "legally wed," "partners for life"—can and do change from couple to couple.

The point of the clause is common sense: it's up to the person officiating at the wedding to make sure everything is in order, and the couple getting married shouldn't be punished for a mistake made by the priest or judge. Article 3, Section 25 has the added effect that if officiants in New York follow their conscience and the constitution, it will be difficult if not impossible for anyone to declare the marriages they perform invalid.

I had originally planned to hold the weddings in the summer of 2004, when the weather was warm and there would be plenty of time to invite the friends and families of those being married. Controversial or not, it was going to be some couple's wedding day, and I wanted them to have the wedding they wanted.

Then on February 4, 2004, the Massachusetts Supreme

Court ruled that same-sex marriages were constitutional
and would be legal in its state. Eight days later, San Francisco's Mayor Gavin Newsom began issuing marriage licenses in City Hall. Thousands of couples were married
in just a few weeks. It was rumored that New Mexico and
Austin, Texas, would follow. Seeing this rising tide of
communities fighting for civil rights, we in New Paltz decided to move up our timetable and not wait for summer.

Same-sex marriage was an issue that New York's Democratic and Republican Party leaders didn't want to touch.
Governor George Pataki needed to stay a moderate to win
reelection as a Republican in a Democratic New York. At
the same time, he was widely seen as angling for a cabinet post in a second Bush presidency. He had to avoid
taking a stand either way or risk losing his chances in
Washington on the one hand, and for the governorship
on the other.

Attorney General Eliot Spitzer, the Democratic
front-runner to unseat Pataki, was avoiding the issue
too. Gay and lesbian civil rights groups had been asking
Spitzer for an opinion on the legality of same-sex marriage for two years, but his office had refused to issue

one. It was obvious Spitzer feared that taking a stance might cost him the governorship.

Into the deafening silence from major New York politicians, President George W. Bush announced he would seek a constitutional amendment to ban gay marriage: "If we are to prevent the meaning of marriage from being changed forever, our nation must enact a constitutional amendment to protect marriage in America." Bush argued that marriage could not "be severed from its cultural, religious, and natural roots without weakening the good influence of society." He would be the first president in the history of our nation to try to use a constitutional amendment to restrict instead of expand the rights of the American people.

The first gay couple to be married in San Francisco had been together for fifty years. One woman was eighty-three and the other seventy-nine. If a couple has been together for that long and formed a love that has helped sustain them for half a century, who are we to stop them from getting married if that's what they want to do? Among the twenty-five couples I married, some were young and might start a family. Who are we to stop them from making their family inside a marriage if they want to?

Marriage equality is an issue of basic human rights. In our country, marriage gives us the right, for example, to visit our loved ones in the hospital if they're dying. Long after everyone else has been forced to leave, you can sit by your husband or wife through the night. It's an act of cruelty to deny that comfort to two people who have been the bedrock of each other's lives.

Civil unions aren't the answer. Many hospital staff won't recognize them and refuse to let in anyone but a married spouse. That is only one flaw amid many. In most states, civil unions do not allow a same-sex spouse to inherit a dead spouse's belongings if there is no will—as married opposite-sex partners can do. Most civil unions do not provide social security benefits for a same-sex survivor. Such dramatic inequities repeat themselves across the country. Vermont's civil unions are the most comprehensive: over a thousand laws that regulate marriage were amended to include civil unions, so that the two would be equal. They aren't equal, though, if one partnership is called marriage and the other a civil union. It's as if certain people aren't good enough to be called married, though they provide the exact same kind of love and loyalty to their partners as married people do. And as good as a Vermont civil union gets, it's inadequate since it will not be recognized in many other parts of the United States.

We've tried separate but equal before in this country. It didn't work then, and it won't work now. Marriage has a cultural weight and a spiritual importance in America that can't be replicated by giving the same rights under a different name. To limit same-sex couples to civil unions is to admit that they have a relationship but insist that their relationship is less than or inferior to the relationships enjoyed (or suffered) by their heterosexual friends and neighbors.

Those who would base the right to marriage not on two people's love for each other but on the gender of those involved betray marriage itself. After all, what is a marriage? Whether or not we're married or ever want to be, I think we all agree that marriage is, in the words of one Dutch minister, "the act of making public what is already written in two people's hearts." No one would deny that the commitment to take care of another human being under any conditions lies at the heart of marriage;

this commitment has absolutely nothing to do with the gender of those involved.

I've been told there's no comparison between the civil rights movement of the sixties and this civil rights movement we are in now. But those who would deny the right of gays to marry would have forced Rosa Parks to the back of the bus. Some blacks are offended to see their suffering equated with that of homosexuals: gays, they say, aren't discriminated against like blacks in the South, gays are not systematically lynched or denied the right to vote, and so on. But while the scale of oppression is undeniably different, the patterns of discrimination are the same. I got a letter from a lesbian police officer in the South thanking me for the marriages in New Paltz and confessing that she has never come out and couldn't tell me her last name for fear that people in her town would find out she was gay and she'd be fired or worse. I got a letter of thanks from a gay couple in Los Angeles who said they'd just been evicted from their apartment because their landlord had found out they were gay. And then there's Matthew Shepard.

In 1998, Matthew Shepard was going to college in Wyoming when some guys at a bar found out he was gay.

By the time someone found him, eighteen hours later, tied naked to a barbed wire fence, he resembled a scarecrow with blood all over its face. He had been lured out of the bar by two young men who'd decided to make Matthew pay for being different. They brought him to a remote area, tied him to a fence, tortured and pistol-whipped him, then left him for dead in near-freezing temperatures.

In July of 2004 I spoke at a fund-raiser for the East End Gay Organization on Long Island, along with Judy Shepard, Matthew's mother. Judy Shepard has spent the years since her son's murder raising money for the Matthew Shepard Foundation and traveling the country urging people to come out of the closet—especially older gay and lesbian people who, as role models, could help reassure younger people grappling with their sexuality— help them refuse to live in shame or fear.

The scale of racism is different, the problem is the same. People are being humiliated, harassed, beaten, and killed in this country simply for being who they are.

Today nearly a third of young black men are either in prison, have come out of prison, or are on their way into prison. After four hundred years of making white people rich by their free or underpaid labor, blacks in much of

America got the right to vote only a generation ago. Many blacks make less money than equally qualified whites at the same job; many blacks are denied mortgages because of their race; certain rental apartments are off limits to them due to racial redlining; and when there's an unsolved crime, the suspect is nearly always automatically a black man. Unless, of course, the crime involved a bomb; then the suspect is first and foremost a Muslim or Arab, as in the Oklahoma City bombing, where the picture of two Middle Eastern men as prime suspects was on the evening news for days until the networks had to admit that it was a white, decorated veteran and his friends who had committed the crime.

It's easy, being white, to forget all this. Because of an accident of my birth, chances are I'll get paid more than anyone else who isn't white for doing the same work. I'll be promoted first and spoken to automatically with respect. Other white people don't get nervous when I'm walking behind them at night. If I wear a hood and baggy pants, no one assumes I'm violent or crosses the street to avoid passing me or avoids looking me in the eye. My whiteness gives me a power and a privilege I was born into and often don't even know I have.

Because I was born a man and not a woman, I'm not afraid someone will slip something into my drink. Chances are I'll get paid more than women for doing the exact same thing they do, and will be hired first and promoted first; I won't be spoken down to and won't have someone staring at my chest when I'm talking to him. I can be pretty sure that when I get a job, it's because of my skills and not because someone wants to sleep with me. My worth will be judged more on my intelligence and abilities than on how thin or beautiful I am.

Because I was born straight and not gay, I'll never know what it is like to go through the tortures of adolescence knowing I'm supposed to like girls but fantasizing about boys. I'll never know what it's like to go through middle school, where the most cutting thing you can be called is "faggot," and know it really does apply to me. I'll never know what it's like to try to find love, knowing only a very small number of the people I'm attracted to would even consider sleeping with me, not because I'm unattractive, but because the thought of sex with men is uninteresting to them at best and at worst disgusts them.

I'll never fear being lynched, beaten, or raped for who I am.

It's easy for bigoted whites to target blacks; it's easy for sexist men to target women. You can see if someone's white or black or a woman. It's not so easy to tell if someone is gay or straight. Their ability to hide may be what makes gay people's suffering appear voluntary and minor to some: if you don't want trouble, all you have to do is shut up and pretend you're someone you're not. But as anyone who has tried knows, denying your true self to satisfy someone else leads to depression and despair. It's no wonder the attempted suicide rate for gay youth is two to three times higher than for heterosexual youth. Scorn, threats, and hate crimes are forcing people to forgo their rights under the American Constitution's provision for freedom and the pursuit of happiness.

Because blacks or Asians or Native Americans are distinguishable on sight, they suffer a much higher degree of discrimination than homosexuals. No one will ever be pulled over for driving while gay. But human injustice has no place in America, overt or not. So long as we accept our neighbors' intolerance of gays, so long as we allow gays to be only partially equal citizens, so long as we elect a president who condemns gays to secondary citizenship, we are contributing to a culture of fear and hate.

As Dr. Martin Luther King, Jr. said, "Injustice anywhere
is a threat to justice everywhere."

*   *   *

Within days of the weddings I performed in New Paltz,
I would face two separate lawsuits.

The Ulster County district attorney charged me with
twenty-four counts of solemnizing weddings without
first being presented with a marriage license. A mis-
demeanor, each count carried a maximum sentence of
a thousand-dollar fine and a year in jail. Though I married twenty-five couples, the DA. only had evidence of
twenty-four.

At almost the same time, Attorney General Eliot
Spitzer finally came out with an opinion on gay marriage. New York law, he argued, should recognize as legal
same-sex marriages from other jurisdictions, such as
Canada, Massachusetts, or Holland, but does not currently allow for same-sex marriage to take place in New
York. Months later Spitzer would argue more broadly
that the equal protection clause of the New York State
Constitution did not apply to same-sex couples.

Days after my criminal charges and the attorney general's opinion were made public, village board member Bob Hebel teamed up with Liberty Counsel, a law firm founded by Jerry Falwell that fights to prevent gays from having equal rights all over the country. Liberty Counsel sued to overturn the Massachusetts Supreme Court decision, for instance, as well as to have the San Francisco marriages annulled. Bob Hebel claimed he was not anti-gay, he simply thought I had broken the law and should be punished. Weeks later, however, he told the *New Paltz Times*, "I do not want to see New Paltz become the gay capital of the world," and was therefore suing me and the village.

The county court judge put a temporary restraining order on me to prevent me from solemnizing more weddings that weekend. Eventually the order would be made permanent. Restraining orders are only issued when there is "immediate and irreparable harm" that would likely come about without one. They make perfect sense in domestic abuse cases. It was hard, though, for me to imagine how marrying consenting parties could cause immediate and irreparable harm to anyone. On this point, Judge J. Michael Bruhn's imagination was more flexible and colorful than mine. If I continued to marry gay couples, he said, there would be a breakdown of the social order, anarchy, and chaos. He said that we can't have elected officials deciding on their own when a law is constitutional or not. The nearly hundred and fifty years of case law upholding an elected executive's right to interpret the New York State Constitution he's sworn to uphold—and to refuse to execute a law he finds unconstitutional—didn't sway Judge Bruhn, or Judge E. Michael Kavanaugh after him, who upheld Bruhn's decision on appeal.

The restraining order was issued a week after I had married twenty-five couples and a day before I was set to perform another round of weddings. I thought for a long time about violating the order, forcing the police to send me to jail. I concluded that going to jail would likely get me more publicity personally but wouldn't do much good for the couples who wanted to get married. Going to jail would put the focus on me instead of on the issues at hand, and it would keep me from working on all the other things I needed to do for the village. I had hoped that one of the thousands of other elected officials in New York would follow in our footsteps once we had shown it could be done, but not a single other New York official outside

New Paltz would solemnize same-sex marriages. Weeks later Deputy Mayor Rotzler and Village Trustee Walsh would join dozens of clergy to solemnize weddings until a restraining order was placed on them too.

Rev. Kay Greenleaf of Poughkeepsie was the first of the more than thirty clergy in half a dozen denominations who would come to New Paltz to keep solemnizing marriages after I was stopped. One evening we sat in my office to go over the legalities of same-sex marriage. Kay's support boosted my spirits. "The God that I know," she said, "doesn't pick and choose. We are all equal in the eyes of God." Two days later she and Rev. Dawn Sangrey continued the weddings—thirteen in all. For their efforts on behalf of civil rights, District Attorney Don Williams charged them each with thirteen misdemeanors. In a fiercely written decision, Judge Judith M. Reichler dismissed their charges:

I find that "tradition" is not a legitimate state interest . . . Slavery was also a traditional institution . . . Same-sex relationships are based on the same thing as heterosexual unions: intimacy, companionship, love, family. Prohibiting same-sex couples from marrying suggests that marriage is about nothing but sex. This is demeaning to all couples who seek to marry and to the institution of marriage.

My arraignment on criminal charges a week later was brief. I sat between my lawyers, Joshua Rosenkranz of Heller Ehrman, in New York City and Andy Kossover, a New Paltz attorney advising Joshua on local legal conditions. Joshua had founded the Brennan Center to provide free legal service for cases that appeared to have significant social impact. Because he'd agreed to represent me, and Andy gave his advice pro bono, the Village of New Paltz would never pay a penny in legal fees related to the marriages. Through the closed doors of the courthouse, we could hear a crowd of over a thousand supporters outside singing, cheering, and chanting, as a brass band played "The Battle Hymn of the Republic." I pled not guilty.

To argue my case, Josh discussed how the issue of gay marriage paralleled the issue of marriage rights for blacks in the South. In Virginia, for example, it was illegal for a white and a black to marry until the late 1960s. Joshua wove old court decisions for racial intermarriage into our argument in favor of marriage rights for everyone.

Judge Jonathan Katz ruled in our favor, saying that

*the law defining the violation charged is unconstitu-
tional . . . this record contains no evidence tending to
show that there is a legitimate state interest in refusing marriage to same-sex partners.*

This was the first time a New York judge ruled that the
state's marriage law violates the federal and state constitutions by refusing same-sex couples the right to marry.
In his ruling, Judge Katz quoted the late Supreme Court
justice Louis Brandeis, "We must be ever on our guard
lest we erect our prejudices into legal principles."

The conservative press and District Attorney Williams
called me names to try to belittle the magnitude of what
we, hundreds of us together, had accomplished. I was the
"boy mayor," "flaky," "brash," and "immature." The *New
York Post* accused me of "plunging the State into needless
confusion" that could cause "irreparable harm." People
also accused me of ambition and of performing the marriages to be in the limelight.

People will believe what they want. This has never
been about me. The attention I got has bolstered my cred-

ibility in some circles, and it's brought threats on my life and slander. The attention was not the point. The point was to use the power I had to force the state to recognize people's human rights. But in the United States, where politicians market themselves like department store products, people have lost faith that any politician could be ambitious to do good, not to become famous and rich.

The real heroes of this or any movement are the un-celebrated people who come home from work and put in the daily, grinding extra hours of steering change in a hu-manitarian direction. Organizations such as ACT UP, PFLAG (Parents, Families and Friends of Lesbians and Gays), high school Gay-Straight Alliances, and thousands of small community organizations all over the country that educate people against homophobia made the mar-riages possible.

The Matthew Shepard Foundation, begun and run by Judy Shepard, provides tools to help us make the United States the safe haven for all and any it was meant to be, to help us live out the commitment to diversity that is written right into our Constitution. If you want to fight bigotry, you might Google the Gay-Straight Al-liance or the Matthew Shepard Foundation to find ways to educate your schools and your community about discrimination and human rights.

A decade ago, when I was in high school, it was controversial in upstate New York to have a Gay-Straight Alliance. Now they're almost everywhere. In an Alliance, high school students and faculty advisors create a space for young people both straight and gay to socialize, away from threats and humiliation. These alliances give young people first dealing with their identity a strong base from which to fight oppression in the brutal social hierarchy of public schools.

Often the place to begin is with ourselves, since we harbor subtle prejudices we aren't even aware of. All of us grow up steeped to some degree in racism, sexism, and homophobia. We need to recognize our own subtle or not so subtle prejudices if we are going to conquer them.

It's never too soon to start promoting diversity. White friends of mine began to educate their daughter, Lucia, when she was a few months old by putting brown skinned and white skinned soft dolls in her crib. When she was older, they put brown and white dolls with doll furniture on a shelf in her room. When Lucia isn't playing with them, the dolls remain on display so she knows that diversity is not simply a noble idea but the perpetual state of the world.

*   *   *

The day after the weddings, a group of us went to dinner at my friends Charles and Maurice's house. There was Billiam—who had been first up, with his partner, Jeffrey, to marry—Rebecca Rotzler, Tom Crampton from the *New York Times,* my sister, Amanda, and my father, Ron. We brought a pile of newspapers with us to look at the pictures and articles that had been written about the previous day's marriages. For a while we told stories and laughed or sighed at the press coverage.

After dinner Charles and Maurice showed us their wedding video. Maurice is a Dutch citizen, and he and Charles had been married years before in Holland. The video was, well, incredibly long. It detailed the civil ceremony before a judge all Dutch couples have, and then the optional religious ceremony afterwards. The couple on the screen were obviously nervous, excited, stunned, and radiantly happy. They were, above all else, in love. There were no passionate speeches about gay rights, no news crews, no op-ed pieces or political discussions. We watched their wedding video the way every wedding video everywhere is watched—the couple narrating the entire thing, remembering stories that didn't make it onto video, the audience sometimes cracking up, sometimes bored to tears, always patient, and often moved.

The risk of criminal prosecution, the marches, the rallies, the controversy were all for this, so that friends and family could sit around a living room and relive a couple's wedding day, without judgment or argument, knowing only the obvious: that these two people are devoted to one another and that their marriage is not a political statement but a relationship. We will have finally won this battle when we are all forgotten. When it becomes as normal for Billiam and Jeffrey or Anya and Lynn to be married as it is normal for women to vote or for America to be a democracy.

None of us is in a position to say that any human being should be restricted in his life, liberty, and pursuit of happiness. None of us has the right to judge other people for the choices they make in pursuing their happiness—so long as those choices don't do harm to others. In a *New York Times* editorial that came out soon after the marriages

I performed, Nicholas Kristof reminded readers that the Defense of Marriage Act was written by thrice-married Representative Bob Barr and signed by the philandering Bill Clinton. "It's less a monument to fidelity," he wrote, "than to hypocrisy."

Those who complain endlessly that gay marriage will destroy the institution of marriage itself should consider the fact that Massachusetts—the only state to approve of gay marriage—has the lowest divorce rate in the country. If you feel threatened by gay marriage, you might ask yourself why. People don't become gay, they're born gay. Homosexuality isn't contagious. People are born gay the same way they're born with freckles or brown hair. If the fear of gay marriage weren't so sad, it would be laughable. It's a tragedy that so many Americans fear other Americans who would do them no harm but would join them, if permitted, in the celebration of human tenderness, mutual respect, and lifelong devotion that marriage is. With our country at war, and a government that looks at the potential for war as a calling card, we have a responsibility, now more than ever, to honor human unity and love whenever given the chance.

Three

Tending Eden

No man can serve two masters; for either he will hate the one, and love the other; or else he will hold to the one, and despise the other. Ye cannot serve God and mammon.

Matthew 6:24

Kevin, John, and I were seventeen when we left school one morning to walk forty-five minutes down half-empty highways and through suburban subdivisions to Albany Airport. We were three of a dozen who showed up to protest the killing of Alaskan timber wolves. Ours was part of a national network of protests designed to hurt Alaskan tourism and get the state's governor to rescind his policy that allowed timber wolf hunting.

We spent a few hours holding hand-painted signs, making up chants and songs, and yelling at people to boycott Alaska. Once we had warmed up to it and overcome our stage fright, it was a lot of fun. But who in

94

their right mind would listen to a dozen environmentalists chanting at them to stay out of Alaska? People had made their travel plans; many had already bought their tickets. They weren't going to thoughtfully read our signs and go to Newfoundland instead. How many were leaving Albany, New York, to go to Alaska anyway?

We were there because we thought it was immoral to exterminate a species for being a nuisance to some people. We were there because we understood that humanity is one part of a larger whole. Only later did I learn that the elimination of a species could be dangerous for the human race.

Chris Fracchia, a local schoolteacher, put it best. He was talking about wetlands, not wolves, but what he said applies to both. In the fall of 2004 our village had a series of public hearings for a proposed wetlands protection law, which got us talking about why wetlands are important. In our temperate climate, one resident explained, wetlands are some of the richest and most diverse ecosystems, the rain forests of the Northeast. Like a sponge, they absorb excess rain and snow, which staves off flooding (a big problem in our village); they can help irrigate farms in a dry spell, keep top soil from eroding, and feed the fish that fishermen rely on to sell. Chris got up and compared our impact on the environment to the game Jenga, where you have a tower of wooden blocks and each player takes turns removing one until the tower collapses. We keep knocking pieces out of our environment, Chris said. Every time we do so and the tower stays up, we think we're fine. But one of these days, we're going to knock a piece out and the whole thing is going to come crashing down.

Whether you think it was created or it evolved or some combination of the two, our world is a complicated latticework of animals, minerals, and plants that rely on each other in ways we don't understand. If we screw around with those interdependencies—by knocking out whole species, for instance—we simply don't know what will happen. We can't predict the results of our own actions.

Some people think that not knowing the consequences of our actions means that those consequences can be ignored. They'll tell you it's necessary to take risks for the sake of "progress." The people who run biotechnology companies are famous for this—take, for example, the executives at Monsanto who spliced a toxic bacteria into corn to produce a plant that contained its own pesticides, without knowing what long term effects this genetic engineering might have on human health or the environment.

We have to ask ourselves if interfering with our environment—by, say, destroying wetlands or killing off Alaskan timber wolves—isn't just immoral but impractical. As New Paltz firefighter Dennis O'Keefe said at our hearings, "Maybe in fifty years we'll find out that all these environmentalists were wrong, that we can destroy wetlands without any impact. But right now we don't know. And I'd rather be on the safe side. If we protect the wetlands now, we'll still have them in fifty years, in case we need them. If we pave them now, and in fifty years discover they're important, we can't knock on someone's front door and tell him, 'Your house was built on a wetland and we need to tear it down to get the wetland back.'"

My friends and I abjectly failed to get this message across at Albany Airport ten years ago. We didn't stop the killing of Alaskan timber wolves, or even slow it down. It would be years before I learned to be effective, not just symbolic, in my efforts to protect the natural world.

*   *   *

97

The media keep telling us we shouldn't really worry about the environment. Every time Fox News or *Time* magazine does a story about the conflict between loggers and those who want to protect the redwoods, they frame the issue as a choice between jobs and trees. It's an either/or scenario. I have to choose whether it's more important to keep loggers logging so they can feed their families or to protect a tree and owl from going extinct. The battle line is drawn, with images of college professors and tattooed kids on one side, and salt-of-the earth laborers on the other. Or there's a developer who wants to build senior housing, and a group of pierced, young protesters trying to save the wetlands where the developer wants to build. The developer says he's interested in the good of the community. Who could possibly argue against senior housing? How can protecting a swamp compete with putting a roof over Grandma's head?

But environmentalism is not an either/or scenario. Environmental policy doesn't stop progress. Protecting the environment creates millions of needed jobs and stimulates our economy. But that's not the point. The point is that our species is simply a part of the world around us. We're not self-sufficient creatures who can strip-mine, clear-cut, and develop whatever and wherever we want to. Every action has a reaction and every piece of the natural world we destroy reduces humanity's well-being.

Given the devastation of poverty in our inner cities and rural areas, given our loss of good-paying, union manufacturing jobs, it may seem selfish and out of touch to care about the environment. But it's a mistake to assume that working Americans don't care about it, that it's an elitist issue, something only people with free time on their hands care about.

Caring about nature isn't just about making sure we have good places to hike, clean streams to fish in, or places to go swimming. It's about preserving our health. Poor and working people, more than the rich, *have* to care about the environment, because we're the ones most hurt by environmental negligence. It is mainly the working class that gets sick from PCBs and radiation, because we live near the factories we work in. It's poor kids who get asthma in huge numbers, because big businesses choose to put the plants that contaminate the air and water in low-rent neighborhoods. The moneyed class decides how and where to destroy nature, then lives as far as possible from the destruction they've wrought. The low-wage worker often has no choice but to live in polluted areas that promote disease. You won't find George Bush or Dick Cheney living a block away from a garbage dump, an airport, or a factory. Their children didn't lie in bed at night coughing up blood, with no health insurance to cover the cost of taking them to the doctor. While callously steeping the children of the poor in toxic chemicals, those in charge of industry, government, and finance use their swollen income to send their own kids to private school and the best doctors.

In time, though, if we don't make fast and serious changes, the average person's crumbling health and wasted environment will spread to the high-end suburban fortresses of American privilege. Let's not hide from what's happening to our natural world: climate change, the destruction of biodiversity, and the depletion of our natural resources affect us all. Let's not shy away from the clear solutions: clean energy, self-reliant communities, and regulations on industry.

* * *

In 1988 an international group of leading scientists formed the Intergovernmental Panel on Climate Change. The IPCC wrote a report with four critical conclusions. Climate change, or global warming, it said, is happening and happening fast; its cause is mainly carbon emissions that result from the coal and oil energy we use in our everyday lives; America emits more carbon into the air than any other nation; and if emissions go unchecked, global warming will destroy human life as we know it within forty-five to seventy-five years.

Never in the history of humankind had so many top scientists united on one issue.

Many countries took the report to heart. They immediately created regulations and research to cut carbon emissions and find ways to manufacture electricity with minimal use of fossil fuels. Wind power, for example, has been growing in Europe at a rate of 40 percent a year.

While European governments began to actively help their industries evolve into a new energy age, President Bush dismissed the Intergovernmental Panel on Climate Change report, calling it "foreign science." The IPCC was, it so happens, composed largely of Americans. When scientists at the U.S. National Academy of Sciences followed Bush's order to produce their own, all-American report, they agreed 100 percent with the international group—and painted an even more frightening picture. Bush ignored them and Congress followed suit.

The U.S. media still report climate change as a debate, setting statements by oil company executives and the ex-oilmen who run the country on equal footing with the words of internationally renowned atmospheric experts. As writer Arundhati Roy has said, "It's important to understand that the corporate media don't just support the neoliberal project. They *are* the neoliberal project. This is not a moral position they have chosen to take; it's structural. It's intrinsic to the economics of how the mass media work."

Media companies are not neutral observers of the world; they have a bias since they are corporations themselves. The vast majority of media are subsidiaries of the very industries they're supposed to monitor. If reporting the whole truth will make their parent companies more money, they'll do it. If, as often happens, reporting only partial truth or lies will make their owners more money, they'll do that too. Media analyst Ben Bagdikian notes that all the major media run twenty years ago by fifty different corporations have now been consolidated into five fiefdoms, each ruled by one man. That's five men running all of television, radio, newspapers, magazines, and books for some 294 million Americans.

A slightly bigger map of corporate media clusters would include General Electric, one of the nation's largest nuclear energy and nuclear weapons contractors—and owner of NBC. This means that on NBC, we rarely if ever see issues surrounding nuclear power presented in a critical way. In fact, when nuclear issues are presented—whether it's plant safety, nuclear waste disposal or depleted uranium used in armor-piercing shells—the nuclear industry is almost always presented in a positive light and antinuclear arguments belittled or overlooked. With a straight face, the media report the findings of scientists *on industry payroll*—findings which of course deny climate change and marginalize reputable scientists who say climate change is real. No matter what your television tells you, though, the mainstream scientific community insists that climate change must be reversed or we might not survive the century.

If this sounds like paranoia, consider that the U.S. Department of Defense thinks climate change is such a threat, it has prepared a national defense policy in case of a new ice age. Our government is spending money to prepare a defense against the very climate change threat they dismiss as "alarmist."

An ice age may result from global warming because the melting of polar ice caps (which has already begun) dilutes the salinity of the Atlantic Ocean. The sea's saltiness is a main factor in keeping us, in the northern hemisphere, warm. This is because a global ocean current that acts like a giant conveyor belt brings warm water from the tropics north. The salt and cold temperature of the North Atlantic make it dense enough to sink, pulling up the warmer water, which, with its warm air currents, gets dragged northward. Melted glacier water will make the North Atlantic less salty, which means less dense. If that water isn't dense enough to sink, it could bring the conveyor belt to a crashing halt. The warm water and air from the tropics would, in this case, stop heating up North America and Europe.

Scientists used to think that an ice age came on slowly, taking thousands of years to build up, but according to the Woods Hole Oceanographic Institute, it may come on quickly—in a matter of just three or four years.

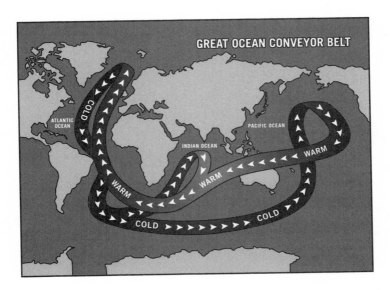

While the oil companies are right that there have been ice ages before, never before has an ice age been brought on by the living inhabitants of the planet. Never before has there been the choice either to heed science's warning and convert to new energy sources or to ignore science, put our heads in the sand, and let those glaciers melt in the Arctic only to reappear in the Carolinas.

While we don't know for certain that climate change will kill us, no one knows for certain it won't. What we do know is that our current technologies cause global warming and already leave disease and death in their wake. Eliminating our reliance on fossil fuels will make people safer and healthier, along with preserving the health of our environment. Isn't it better to live a cleaner, healthier life in the short term, while also heading off a possible future disaster?

Scientists may not know whether Mount Saint Helens will erupt again, but is their uncertainty a reason to build a city on the volcano? Doesn't it make sense to plan for the worst and hope for the best?

It's fair to say that given the choice, most of us would choose to get our home heating and car fuel from sources that don't pollute, such as solar, wind, and geothermal. But we most often don't have that choice. Businesses make that choice for us through their investment, research, and development policies. Governments make that choice for us with their trade agreements, land use laws, tax incentives, and subsidies. They choose oil, coal, and nuclear power. They *choose* to make the human race sick and our resources scarce; they *choose* to risk fatal climate change.

According to the Environmental Protection Agency, America gets almost half of its electricity from coal-burning power plants. Most of the rest comes from gas and nuclear plants. If we're getting almost all of our energy from lethal sources, it's not because the market has spoken and consumers prefer their electricity complete with nuclear waste and carbon emissions; it's because oil company executives and nuclear power companies have invested their capital in the resource that brings the most dividends to their stockholders. That resource is members of the U.S. Congress.

As long as we allow our economy and political institutions to be run by those who make the most money, nothing will change. We need a cooperative energy industry that is kept on a tight leash by a nonprofit, democratic government. Were Congress to write trade laws that punished industry for causing pollution anywhere in the world, or liability laws that forced companies to clean up the poisons they dump on our communities and pay sufficient reparations, we would see fewer oil spills, and fewer toxic pesticides leaching into our drinking water and rivers. While there are laws on the books that would force cleanup, they're riddled with loopholes and regulatory hurdles that make enforcement difficult, if not impossible. It doesn't do any good to call for more enforcement of laws designed to be evaded. That's like being given a car whose spark plugs are designed to fall out, then blaming the mechanic for not being able to fix it.

Congress could write laws to make it highly profitable to produce our energy with clean, renewable sources rather than deadly nuclear material, coal, and oil, but they don't want to. We could run our country on decentralized wind, solar, and hydrogen energy. We could retrain nuclear and coal-fired power plant workers to manufacture, install, and maintain a power supply that doesn't poison their kids. We could fund college engineering programs to train people to work in solar rather than nuclear energy and work with organizations like the Oil, Chemical and Atomic Workers Union (OCAW) to develop job training for semiskilled or unskilled workers in the newly subsidized industries. The U.S. government could give the billions of free dollars it gives to oil, coal, and nuclear power companies, and to energy traders such as Enron, to locally owned, cooperative solar collection networks, wind farms, and hydrogen-based energy plants. It could, but it doesn't. Why? Because the Enrons of the world have invested millions of dollars in the campaigns of the politicians who make environmental policy. There's a lot of money to be made

in keeping things the way they are. We won't get clean
energy until we eliminate the profit in dirty energy.

Ravaging the environment, as we are doing, has mul-
tiple consequences, one of which is war. Scientists are
beginning to see, for instance, that in just a few years
fresh water will become more valuable than gold, and
wars across the world will be fought over access to clean
water. In her acceptance speech for the 2004 Nobel
Peace Prize, Wangari Muta Maathai said that development and deforestation in Africa had created a dearth of
clean drinking water, firewood, balanced diets, shelter,
and income. "There can be no peace," she explained,
"without equitable development; and there can be no
development without sustainable management of the
environment in a democratic and peaceful space." People fight for scarce resources: now it's oil; soon it will be
water. A grassroots organizer for decades, Maathai spent
time in prison for repeatedly protesting Kenya's one-
party political system. When free elections were finally allowed, she formed the Kenyan Green Party and promptly
won election to the national parliament. Appointed
deputy minister of the environment, Maathai has worked
on environmental issues for the last thirty years. To her

Nobel audience, she also said, "God created the planet from Monday to Friday. On Saturday he created human beings. The truth of the matter is . . . if man was created on Tuesday . . . he would have been dead on Wednesday, because there would not have been the essential elements that he needs to survive." The depletion of our natural resources is as detrimental to us as climate change, and it must be stopped.

Clearly, not all rich people and corporations are responsible for the environmental problems we're facing. Look at Robert Kennedy Jr., who created the environmental watchdog organization Riverkeeper to clean up and protect the Hudson River. Then there's Arianna Huffington, a political writer who ran for governor of California in 2003. A wealthy socialite and former Republican, she now uses her fortune against her class interests and in favor of the rest of us. Sean "Puffy" Combs has funded massive voter registration and education efforts. Then, of course, there's Ralph Nader, who sued Detroit auto manufacturers and used the settlements from his lawsuits to found hundreds of public interest organizations, many of them pro-environment.

A few corporations have proven that substantial profits

and protecting the environment can go hand in hand. Ben & Jerry's ice cream works with the Working Assets phone company, for example, which reinvests some of its profits into educating the public and lobbying against political corruption and environmental destruction. If all corporations functioned with the social conscience of a Ben & Jerry's, maybe we could live out the congressional dream of an unregulated free-market economy. The fact is, though, most corporate CEOs are only interested in making money and won't voluntarily spend a dollar, let alone a million, to take care of the resources that made them rich in the first place. With rare exceptions, corporations are designed to maximize profit no matter the human cost, and the wealthy, by upbringing and education, are trained to protect and expand their wealth.

* * *

It's up to us, then—the people who suffer most immediately from environmental abuse—to come up with solutions. But it's easy to get overwhelmed at the immensity of environmental problems that need solving. It's hard to feel as if you're doing any good. No matter how many aerosol cans you aren't using, the ozone hole gets bigger. Global warming is happening and there's nothing you can do about it, so why not get the SUV instead of the car with better mileage? It's easy to get discouraged because it's hard to think of something we can do that will make real, tangible change—beyond writing a letter to the editor and hoping that someone, somewhere will read it and decide to stop polluting. Doing something that doesn't make a meaningful difference can demoralize us as much as doing nothing at all.

To make real environmental improvements, we need to do no less than reimagine the very layout of our lives. Our towns and cities are designed to add to global warming because they are not self-sufficient. Our food needs to be brought in, our sewage taken out; we have to transport ourselves to work or shop. The best strategy for short- and medium-term environment protection is to make our communities self-reliant.

Suburban sprawl, the predominant American landscape, spreads people over large tracts of land located on the periphery of downtown. This means that most people have to drive to work; they don't have the option to walk or bike. In most parts of the United States, public transportation has broken down completely or runs so inefficiently that people don't bother with it: their own car is faster and easier than a train.

Consider, too, that the food we eat is grown across the country or in some other country and flown or driven thousands of miles to reach our local grocery store or bodega. The more fossil fuel we burn to get to work, get our food, and get around, the more contaminated we make our air and water.

One way to take responsibility for global warming is to redesign our own towns and villages. It isn't as hard as it sounds. With the help of our town boards, we can write zoning laws that require developers to build mixed-use buildings, with commercial space on the ground floor and two or three stories of housing above. Developers, for instance, could retrofit existing strip malls or revive abandoned ones by adding a few stories of housing on top. We could create neighborhoods where we would live in walking or biking distance of our workplace.

The American Journal of Health Promotion recently devoted an entire issue to "Health-Promoting Community Design." Clearly, the American epidemic of obesity, with its backseat illnesses, is linked to sprawl, where people never walk but always drive. The point is not to take away people's cars but to make them optional. Ideally, we wouldn't need our car to fulfill our every need. If we could walk to the grocery store, walk to work, walk to the bookstore, laundromat, or pizzeria, it's doubtful we would drive there. We'd save our car for long-distance drives.

If more people lived in walkable communities, they'd not only feel better, they'd drastically reduce carbon fumes from gasoline. A whole movement of planners, architects, and builders is dedicated to environmentally sound, community-enhancing, health-promoting development. Organizations like the Congress for the New Urbanism and the Pace University Land Use Law Center are writing templates of better zoning laws to serve municipalities. The groundwork is there, waiting for local officials to make use of it.

Another way to make our communities more self-sufficient is to grow our own food. By growing our own food, we keep thousands of tons of emissions from trucking and refrigeration out of the atmosphere, and we build a stronger community.

Huguenot Street Farm in New Paltz is a prime example. The farm comprises seventy acres on the east bank of the Wallkill River in the heart of New Paltz. Instead of growing acres of one crop for export, as corporate farms do, Ron and Kate Khosla are pioneering new ways to farm that involve diverse crops. Without using any pesticides, they grow dozens of organic and heirloom fruits and vegetables. These crops are descendants of rare and specialized plants whose seeds have been saved at each harvest for the next planting, from generation to generation.

Instead of selling its produce to fancy restaurants or grocery store chains, Huguenot Street Farm sells its produce directly to the local community. It works like this: a person pays the farm a few hundred dollars a year (depending on what size share you get) in exchange for a few bags of produce every week of the growing season. By selling dozens or hundreds of shares, the farmers get the money they need up front to cover costs for the coming year without taking all the financial risk themselves: if there's a bad crop or drought or cold snap, then the entire membership of the cooperative takes a part of the hit. I'm willing to take that small risk rather than force individual farmers to go under from one bad season.

Every week I go to the farm and pick up a few bags of locally grown, organic produce for the same price as or less than what I would pay in a grocery store for produce soaked in pesticides and trucked across the country or flown across the world. Pickup day at the farm is one of the best events of the week, with hundreds of people who might not otherwise see each other chatting, playing with each other's kids, and simply building a stronger community.

Shipping and storing produce leaves a trail of environmental damage and human rights abuse that ends with the diesel fumes behind the shipping trucks and refrigerants and begins with the underpaid migrant farm workers, who, on top of suffering long hours, criminally low pay, and brutal working conditions, are in many places prevented by law from forming a union. Being a member of a CSA (community-supported agriculture) farm like Ron and Kate's allows you to get fresh produce untainted by the environmental and human rights abuses that go into delivering almost every carrot to the shelves of the local ShopRite.

There are still more things we can do to improve our environmental conditions, if we're willing to get involved with grassroots projects that aren't glamorous but make a real difference. A few years ago, for instance, I read an article in a local newspaper about John Jankiewicz. Superintendent at the water treatment plant in Lloyd, New York, John spearheaded an innovative way for municipalities to treat sewage with reed beds. When I was elected, a reed bed system was one of the first projects I wanted to start in our village.

While human waste may not be a scintillating topic at the dinner table, it's a vital one to address if you want a clean, safe environment. In our village, until recently, all human waste ended up at our central sewage plant. After being filtered and treated, it had all the water squeezed out of it, was loaded into trucks, and was driven across New York State to a dump in the Rochester area. As the years went by and landfills filled up, we had to drive our sludge farther and farther away. Not only did we have to pay the dumps and landfills to take it, but we had to pay more and more money to cover the costs of the trucks, drivers, fuel, maintenance of vehicles, and so on.

John had read about reed beds but didn't believe they would work. He spent six years experimenting with them and surprised himself. They treated waste effectively in his own community—which was far better than shipping it out to someone else's backyard to mix with other garbage and become toxic.

Reed bed systems are simple: you plant a bed of common reeds (in our case, phragmites, but you can use cattails or others) and dump waste directly onto them. Since reed stems are hollow like straws, they bring oxygen down, helping bacteria grow that then digest the waste. The reeds break it down with no odor, no chemicals, and no machines. There's no pollution from trucks driving across the state, no landfill fees, no toxic chemicals to pollute the groundwater.

Our first reed bed was planted in the summer of 2003 at a cost of roughly twelve thousand dollars. Once the reeds reach maturity, that one bed will treat 30 percent of our village's waste, breaking it down to fertilizer we can use on our lawns. When we add up all the costs for landfill usage, we'll be saving almost ten thousand dollars a year. After a decade, we'll harvest the composted waste and the reeds and plant another bed, using the compost for landscaping. We plan to take the money we're saving with the first bed to build a second and third, so that within just a few years, our village will be treating almost all of its waste in-house, without pollution. When the system's finished, it will save nearly thirty thousand dollars of taxpayer money annually, while at the same time keeping hundreds of tons of human waste out of landfills.

As with mixed-use urban design and CSA farms, reed beds meet basic human needs within our own community. Self-sufficiency will wean us off our reliance on other countries for their oil; an American life that is self-reliant is less expensive and less prone to terrorism, as many terrorists have made it clear that the less we have to do with them, the less they have against us. Given our history as proud, resourceful pioneers, we should jump at the chance to become more independent.

Yet another form of self-reliance is to start your own local power company and kiss corporate utilities good-bye. In certain states, local communities can, by law, form municipal power companies. They can do this through their town board or city council. Communities in the Pacific Northwest and cities such as Cleveland own and operate their own system of power plants and have the authority to decide how they produce their energy. Many are choosing greener methods.

Here in New York, making your own energy can be as

simple as buying it. The New York State Power Authority is required to sell electricity to municipal power companies at wholesale rates. Right now your electric bill—if it's from a private utility such as Con Edison—pays for unnecessary expenses like exorbitant CEO salaries, stock market speculation, mergers and acquisitions, and marketing campaigns. In other words, you're getting charged every month not only for the power you use but for profit-making schemes and an executive's house in the Bahamas. A locally run power company, though, only needs to cover its basic costs: the power it provides, office space, and a reasonably salaried staff. If the company's costs are low, so is your bill. If you want to do something to help the environment but don't know what, consider approaching your city council about forming your own power company. You'll make your neighbors' bills go down and be in a better position to choose a wind or solar source.

Clean energy would function very well in the United States, and there are state-run agencies—albeit poorly funded—setting out to prove it. The New York State Energy Research and Development Authority (NYSERDA), for instance, offers small incentives to homeowners and local governments to promote alternative energy. In the summer of 2003, NYSERDA awarded our village a grant to install a solar panel array on our Village Hall. The hundred thousand dollars we got, along with fifty thousand dollars from the village and the Town of New Paltz, can pay for a system that will save the village nearly nine thousand dollars a year in electricity costs. Our savings will allow us to buy more solar panels, and with more panels going up every year, our community buildings will see a steadily shrinking electricity bill, saving taxpayer money. The fact is, contrary to popular thought, alternative energy costs *less* than oil, coal, and nuclear power.

Wind power too, with effort, can be woven into a clean energy network. The nonprofit New York Public Interest Research Group and the company NewWind Energy are selling wind power to the average household or small business for an additional two to three cents per kilowatt, which translates into an extra five dollars or so a month. Part of the five bucks helps finance the construction of more windmills on farms in places such as the Great Plains or central New York. The host farmer is paid to allow a windmill to be built on his land, helping to subsidize the farm and keep it going in hard times.

In America, all electricity produced goes into a central pot—the electrical grid. The more wind power premiums we pay, the higher the percentage of the grid power will come from windmills, instead of from nuclear or coal plants. For sixteen thousand dollars, the Village of New Paltz could subsidize the same amount of wind power into the grid as we currently take out, effectively buying one hundred percent of our electricity from wind farms. It's a win-win situation, with struggling New York farmers making money on the windmills they allow on their land, and our dependency on nuclear and fossil fuels reduced.

While nuclear power plants do create jobs, these jobs are all concentrated; you need to live near a plant to work at one. If Congress subsidized solar and wind power instead of nuclear, thousands of new jobs would be created all across the country, rather than clustered around power plants. We could replace our ugly, ominous nuclear plants with small, decentralized solar networks in every city, town, and village in America. People would be trained in the installation, maintenance, and design of solar panels, putting local communities in charge of safe, clean energy with no byproducts. Factories would be built to manufacture parts. With every community in the country buying, installing, and maintaining the panels, solar energy would be a huge boost to American manufacturing.

What else can we do?

We can get the millions of cars on our roads running on cleaner fuel. While the big car companies advertise green car prototypes that a few movie stars drive to the Academy Awards, none is putting a really clean car into production at the rate needed to make a difference. If we wait for them to give us clean-exhaust vehicles, they'll have to outfit them for glaciers, as the next ice age will already have come.

In the late nineteenth century, Rudolf Diesel invented an engine that would run on low-grade oils. Intended to revolutionize agriculture, the Diesel was originally designed to run on peanut oil. Farmers would grow a few acres of peanuts to be pressed into oil that could be used as fuel for their combines, harvesters, and transport trucks. The Diesel would liberate farmers from the railroads' obscenely high freight rates.

The eighteen-wheelers on our highways don't run on peanut oil today because the oil companies redesigned

Diesel's engine to run on a dirty byproduct called petrodiesel fuel, or just plain "diesel." With a few modifications, though, your diesel engine could still run on many types of low-grade oil, and one of the best is vegetable oil. To use it, you would simply have to replace your car's rubber hoses with ones that wouldn't deteriorate. And if you live in a cold climate, you would add a second fuel tank, a second set of fuel lines, and a toggle switch on the dash to flush out the tank with petrodiesel before leaving it to sit in the cold. Diesel fuel gels to the consistency of petroleum jelly in the cold, and vegetable oil gels at a higher temperature than diesel fuel.

For those of us who don't want to deal with adding fuel tanks and hoses, there's biodiesel. Biodiesel, a vegetable-based fuel (usually soy), has all the benefits of vegetable oil without the need for engine or tank conversions. For about three dollars per gallon, you can buy it by mail from small manufacturers around the country. Biodiesel's high cost is made up for by the added fuel efficiency of diesel engines and the dramatic drop in pollution when you use it. And the cost is likely to go down as regular gas prices climb and fuel manufacturers start to mass-produce biodiesel. Already the commercial automobile industry is beginning to design cars for biodiesel; for instance, the new DaimlerChrysler Jeep Liberty, a midsize SUV, runs on a biodiesel blend that gives 30 percent better fuel efficiency than gasoline and reduces greenhouse gas emissions by 20 percent.

Reed beds, community-supported agriculture, decentralized clean energy, and biodiesel fuel are good short- and medium-term projects that will slow global warming. But they're limited. For long-term solutions, we need a functioning democracy to reign in business to meet the needs of the American people.

*   *   *

Free-market advocates tell us to trust private industry to do the right thing. It's had five hundred years to do the right thing. It hasn't and it won't. Executives in the energy and agribusiness industries take home millions of dollars a year, plus benefits and expenses. They pay lobbyists hundreds of millions to tug the collar they keep around government's neck. "Trust us, we'll take care of you," says private industry. That same industry hides scientific studies from the public to increase profits; that same industry finances political campaigns to make sure it gets deregulated; it would rather pay politicians than pay for health, safety, and environmental protections. Life-and-death decisions are made every day by corporate paper pushers—our life and our death—and if there's money to be made in death, industry pays Congress for a license to kill. Ben & Jerry's aside, neither industry nor the governments they buy have a conscience.

Scientists say that emissions need to be cut by 70 percent within this decade if we are even to hope to reverse climate change. Global warming won't hurt us in three hundred or even one hundred years, they say; it's hurting us now. Ten thousand people on the island nation of Tuvalu have to relocate because of the rising sea level. In the United States, mosquitoes are suddenly infesting Barrow, Alaska, where there have never been mosquitoes, because the temperature has risen about seven degrees in the last thirty years. Three devastating hurricanes blew into Florida all in one month of 2004. The higher sea level, the sudden mosquito invasion, and the increased storms are no accident; they're the result of global warming.

*   *   *

United Nations weapons inspector Hans Blix, famous for his efforts to bring Iraq into compliance with UN resolutions, said in the spring of 2003, "To me the question of the environment is more ominous than that of peace and war . . . I'm more worried about global warming than I am of any major military conflict."

We don't live on a melting Arctic glacier. We don't live in the ocean, where the entire marine food chain is being devastated by heat stress. We may not live in Canada, where the frozen tundra is thawing and releasing methane and carbon dioxide gases into the atmosphere.

But the Arctic glacial thaw is changing the temperature and salinity of the entire Atlantic Ocean, so that not only is the conveyor belt of warm air currents we rely on at risk, the fish we eat won't survive. According to Pulitzer-winning climate expert Ross Gelbspan, when gases from the tundra drive Canadian communities south for health reasons, we Americans may be faced with refugees looking for jobs in our neighborhood. While some parts of the world freeze, others will undergo heat waves and drought. Crops under heat stress

demand more water—water we won't have in part because we'll have built malls over our wetlands. When the
crops don't pan out, we'll suffer malnutrition and the
sicknesses that go with it. Starvation will no longer be reserved for the world's poor. And bad crops will make the
world's poor even worse off, driving more people to join
terrorist organizations as the only effective way to
change course. And the terrorists will have a good case
against us: it will be our denial and negligence—all the
steps to reverse global warming that we refused to take—
that will have brought on their suffering. Climate change
will hurt every one of us in every part of the globe, no
matter how much money we make or how many prayers
we say.

*   *   *

How do we take on the CEO of Westinghouse? How do
we fight greed and irresponsibility on a scale like this? I
don't have the time or energy to uselessly bang my fist on
a wall that won't move. Neither do you. When we sign a
petition to shut down a nuclear plant, or demonstrate
outside Indian Point, who's listening? Imagine that Mr.

Burns from *The Simpsons* looks down from his office at twenty people with handmade signs and old chants, and says, "OK, OK! I give up! You're right, nuclear power is wasteful, dangerous, and expensive!" I don't think so.

Protests and demonstrations aren't for the Mr. Burnses of the world, they're for us. Protests give us hope and unity, but they don't scare our enemies anymore. We can write letters to Congress, newspapers, and corporations. We can march and chant. But the millions of letters sent over the last few years, with the help of organizations such as MoveOn.org, didn't stop Dick Cheney from inviting coal and oil industry executives into his office to shape environmental policy. Letters didn't stop Cheney from peeling back coal emission regulations or give a spine to the Democrats to stand up to him. Millions of people marching all over the world on February 15, 2003, didn't stop Bush from invading Iraq or stop Congress from giving Bush the power to declare war wherever and whenever he sees fit.

Protests that might multiply and escalate into more militant action or civil disobedience could force decision makers to change policy to prevent more unrest. The demonstrations and marches for civil rights and, later,

Vietnam are perfect examples. Nowadays though, with cities requiring protestors to stage their event like a movie, and with protestors sequestered in cages on the edge of town, where television cameras can easily avoid them, it's very hard to demonstrate with much force. This isn't to say that protesting is useless, but it usually serves the organizers—energizing and consolidating them—more than hurts their opponents. While it used to be a powerful tactic of coercion, most demonstrating has been tamed into a genteel effort to persuade.

Greed cannot be stopped with persuasion. We won't win democracy just because it's a good idea. With all our short- and medium-term grassroots solutions, we still need to take back our country. The tactic of persuasion assumes the people you're trying to persuade don't know they are causing harm. But Exxon knew that reducing safety features to save money would result in more oil spills, inevitably on the scale of the Exxon *Valdez*; the company preferred to save money than to prevent them. General Electric knew for years that it was pouring dangerous PCBs into the Hudson River—PCBs that would generate cancer and brain damage in the surrounding working-class communities—but did it anyway. How can we persuade these companies and others like them, if the cruel facts haven't persuaded them already?

We physically stop or threaten to physically stop the harm from being done. While Greenpeace had already begun using direct action, the tactic spread in the late 1970s and early 80s with a handful of staffers at the big environmental groups—the Sierra Club, the Wilderness Society—who were sick of being ignored. They saw their lobbying efforts fail. They were working harder and harder just to slow down the pace of destruction, and they weren't able to reverse much of it.

They left their jobs and founded an organization called Earth First!, dedicated to direct action—that is, to physically stopping the assaults on the Earth instead of trying to persuade corporations and the government to stop them. They took tactics handed down from the labor and civil rights movements and applied them to environmental protection. When old-growth forests were threatened by timber companies, they chained themselves to trees to physically stop those trees from being cut. They destroyed logging roads to prevent the machines from getting to the forests in the first place. They poured sand in the crankcases of bulldozers. As the years went by and chapters of Earth First! spread around the world, some Earth First! organizers went underground to form the Earth Liberation Front (ELF), which would research and systematically pull apart engines of environmental destruction even more thoroughly.

One of the most powerful and unintended consequences of Earth First! and the Earth Liberation Front has been to strengthen the power of the less confrontational organizations they were born from. With the threat of the ELF in the background, the doors to Congress have opened wider to the Sierra Club. Remember, Dr. Martin Luther King, Jr.'s advice was sought by three presidents in part because they preferred to deal with the nonviolent King than with the Deacons of Defense or Malcolm X.

Often environmental debates are not over whether a dam that would destroy dozens of communities and flood a valley should be built; they're over how that dam should be built. Environmental groups will argue that the dam should be built in a way that does the least damage possible, and developers will argue that the dam must be built the cheapest way possible. Since the developers can buy the local politicians and regulators, the argument is lopsided to begin with; often the best that environmentalists can expect is to desperately wring some small concessions from the developer and hope that only most of the local ecology will be destroyed, instead of all of it.

But what if, the year before, a dam got blown up halfway through construction?

All of a sudden, the negotiations take on a different tone. Now the developers know that if they don't work with the environmentalists and the community, they may never build the project no matter how many members of Congress they buy. Now the developers are eager to meet with the "reasonable" environmentalists in order to head off the more militant ones.

Direct action very publicly throws a monkey wrench into the gears of ecological destruction. Julia Butterfly Hill and her support team, for instance, spent two years keeping Hill living in the branches of an ancient redwood tree. For two years the Pacific Lumber Company a subsidiary of Maxxam, tried to bully, threaten, and intimidate Hill into coming down; the company eventually agreed not to cut down the grove if Hill would get out of the tree.

Activists who tear up logging roads make it more expensive to log old-growth forests. Every time a road is washed out, it costs the lumber company money to pay their workers to stand around and do nothing. It costs them money to rebuild the road. It costs them money on the interest and investment potential of the money they're not making. If a local community can drive up the cost of clear-cutting beyond what the company would make by selling the wood it cuts, the company will likely pull out.

The point of this kind of direct action is not to destroy property but to cost the company more money than it would make by cutting down those trees; the point is to save a forest without hurting anyone in the process.

People who are practiced and passionate about one set of tactics too often attack those who use different ones. The organizer who has spent years perfecting the art of direct action writes off the lobbyist as a sellout. The activists who engage in sensitive, difficult negotiations with those in power lose their temper at the direct action organizer who doesn't understand that progress also happens with small steps, delicately managed. What too few realize is how important each can be to the other. The Sierra Club professionals who spend years writing an environmentally sound forestry bill that saves redwoods and local jobs need those people who sit in trees or else their bill won't even get a hearing. The militants need the environmental professionals to make sure that the redwoods they risked their life to save stay saved once the militants leave the woods; each approach is made more powerful by the other.

*   *   *

Voting isn't the only way to make change; neither is direct action. We can't afford to be ideologically committed to any single tactic; we don't have time to be rigid. We need to be ideologically committed to achieving our goals with whatever tactic suits the circumstance, whether it's blowing up a dam, running for office, or meeting with legislators to try to persuade them to do the right thing.

Our job, simply by virtue of our being alive, is to confront any authority that betrays the many for the good of a few. Energy companies, loggers, and big developers are betraying millions of people's health and endangering their lives so a few hundred corporate executives can line their pockets.

Let's use short-term projects like reed beds and

biodiesel to get hands-on experience and prove there are alternatives that work in the real world, not just on paper. At the same time, let's redesign our local electoral laws to encourage full representation in government and a full spectrum of debate on which to base public policy. Let's begin at the local level and work up, retooling our democracy so that those of us most affected by environmental destruction are making the decisions, not raw commercial interests, campaign funders, pollsters, and focus groups.

Environmental movements and pro-democracy movements are natural allies. For environmental work to have long-term success, it needs to incorporate pro-democracy work. Some organizations are already working on both sets of issues simultaneously—the Green Party; the Ruckus Society; an archipelago of independent bookstores, publishers, and magazines. But more bridges need to be built between single-issue organizations such as the Sierra Club and the Center for Voting and Democracy. Memberships and donors to these organizations are already overlapping; the issues simply need to be more formally linked. Imagine, for example, how much better it would be for democracy and the environment both if the

Sierra Club made support for instant runoff voting a condition for their endorsement of a candidate?

Let's methodically create local, practical solutions to our problems. We will experiment and find the ones that work, so that when our government at last sends subsidies for alternative energy and an alternative voting system, we'll be ready to duplicate our methods all across the country. Democracy and environmental health will only flourish from the ground up.

*   *   *

We have a choice between the corporate good and the public good. We have a choice to organize our society either to reward greed or to reward generosity. If we choose greed, only a fraction of us will ever get the American Dream. The reality of life is that most of us are the backs a few ruthless people step on as they climb their way to the top.

Our choice is not between a vow of poverty or a Reaganesque worship of money. We can build a culture of cooperation and sharing where all of us have plenty. There's enough money in the world to reward those who work hard, without creating poverty.

And it's absolutely possible to build a society and infrastructure that meet our needs without destroying the environment. But as long as we leave environmental policy in the hands of politicians obedient to corporate interests, we might as well leave public health laws in the hands of tobacco companies. It is only after we've regained the ability to represent ourselves in Congress, only after we've driven the moneylenders from the temple and designed our electoral laws so the rich are not the only ones who can win office, only after those who represent more than corporate America are making the decisions that govern our country that we will have an honest debate about these life-and-death issues. Only then can we enshrine in our laws that a biodiverse and clean environment is more important than making money.

FOUR

The Eye of the Needle

It is easier for a camel to go through the eye of a needle than for a rich man to enter into the kingdom of God.

Mark 10:25

When I went to check on Buffy, I found her with a drug dealer and his nervous client. She had interrupted them to explain why Episcopal Hospital needed to stay open, and would they please sign her petition? "Oh, shit," I thought. She's gone too far. But the dealer, who'd coldly stared her down until he'd heard her out, all of a sudden smiled and took the clipboard. "'Course I'll sign it," he said. "I was born in that hospital, my momma was born there. We got to keep Episcopal open." He pulled the other guy over, put the clipboard in his hands, and told him to sign.

Episcopal Hospital, in Kensington, Philadelphia, was,

after all, for those two men and their families. In 1999 Kensington was the poorest neighborhood in the state. Episcopal, its only hospital, had been bought by Temple University, famous for purchasing medical treatment facilities only to take the best equipment and employees back to their main, state-of-the-art hospitals and shut down their new acquisitions. If they shut down Episcopal, kids in Kensington who got sick or hurt would have nowhere nearby to go for help.

I was in Kensington with nine other college activists as part of Union Summer, a program created by the AFL–CIO to teach young people basic organizing skills and hopefully steer them to a career as a union organizer. Each summer hundreds of young activists are sent out into the field to get hands-on experience in the labor movement.

We were in North Philly helping Health Professionals and Allied Employees (HPAE)—the nurses' and technicians' union—fight both to keep the hospital open and to negotiate a better contract. The nurses at Episcopal in the late nineties didn't join a union, they formed a union from scratch to improve unfavorable working conditions. Too few nurses had been working too many hours. If staffing levels were to go up, chronic overtime to go down, and patients to get the attention and care they needed from well-rested, fully equipped nurses, then the nurses and technicians had to have a voice on the job. They, without a doubt, knew patients' needs best. As a new union, the staff hoped through collective bargaining to pry their employer's attention away from the balance sheet long enough to pay attention to patients' needs. The staff had decided that their hospital should run as a democracy and that unionizing was the best tactic for democratizing a workplace.

Unions are the incarnation of our Bill of Rights where we work. Unionization means that workers take their freedom of speech and freedom of assembly seriously. In most of the jobs we hold, we're told to leave our rights at the door. We don't have the right to talk about unionization without risk of being fired; we can't assemble peaceably without being told to break it up by our boss. In fact, most of the time, the only right we have at work, as labor historian Peter Kellman has pointed out, is the right to quit.

On paper, getting a job is contracting with your boss. You agree to sell a certain number of hours of your life in exchange for money. Your boss agrees to hire you with the understanding that he will pay you less money than the value of the thing you produce, keeping the rest for himself as profit. But there's a huge power disparity in these negotiations, as most of the time, your boss has all the power and you have little or none. Without you, his business won't run and he can't make his profit. You are, in a word, indispensable to him, yet he calls all the shots: tells you when to come in; when to leave; how much you will be paid; when you get a raise; when your pay is cut; whether, if you're a nurse, you'll get enough staff; or if you're a miner, whether the mine shaft will be properly ventilated.

There really is safety in numbers. When all the employees at a business get together, they take on enough power to negotiate with their boss. Unions, at their best, aren't simply organizations you join that then intervene on your behalf; they are the means by which all employees cooperate to collectively decide the conditions of their employment. If the people who work at Wal-Mart decide it's unfair that their boss schedules everyone to work thirty-nine and a half hours every week because he has to pay benefits when you work forty or more, they could threaten the store's profit by refusing to work. But only if they protest as a united front: in other words, only if they unionize. Unfortunately, that hasn't happened yet, as Wal-Mart ferociously fights the formation of unions among its workers.

The image of unions as corrupt bureaucracies with their leaders traveling on Lear jets misrepresents the problem with organized labor today. Yes, there's corruption, but on a minor scale, and far less than in the corporate business world. Where humans exist, so does corruption. It makes no sense to dismiss the very idea of unions simply because of a few bad apples. Nor does it make sense to accuse unions, as a carpenter I once knew did, of destroying American industry. I was sixteen and house painting on summer breaks when one afternoon, as the builders and I broke for lunch, I put on a CD of old labor songs. Dan, a carpenter, responded to the music by saying, "Unions are what ruined this country." How? I asked. By getting workers first the ten-hour, then the eight-hour day? By getting us the weekend off by requiring a forty-hour week? In the 1800s the labor movement fought for and won a public school system. Was it that? Or workers' benefits, social security, and an end to child labor? Dan backpedaled. "Unions used to do good things," he admitted, "but that was a long time ago, when working people were oppressed. We don't need them today."

Yet when we spoke, Dan had been working sixteen to eighteen hours a day, seven days a week for months after discovering his son had leukemia. Without health insurance, he was working brutal hours to earn enough money for his medical bills. That was eleven years ago. Today we still don't have universal health care and many parents still work insane hours to keep their sick children alive—work so much, in fact, they have little or no time to spend with those children. If there weren't so many obstacles to joining a union, Dan might have been spared that grinding work schedule by having the universal health care system the labor movement has been advocating for decades.

As beneficial as unions have been, they've been, over the last fifty years, steadily losing numbers, and with them strength. In the fifties and sixties, a third of American workers belonged to a union. Today only 14 percent do. According to Matt Bai in the *New York Times Magazine*, "The age of automation and globalization, with its 'race to the bottom' among companies searching for lower wages overseas, has savaged organized labor." The other reason

for attrition is, says Bai, "employers' antipathy to unions
and federal laws that discourage workers from demanding
one." Since the 1930s, Congress has passed a series of laws
that make it harder to join a union here than in almost
any other western nation. Workers who try to form a
union can be fired without recourse. Workers can strike,
but because of a 1938 Supreme Court decision (*NLRB v.
Mackay*), corporations may permanently replace them if
they do. If union activists aren't fired outright, they are
forced to have an election where employees vote on
whether to form a union or not. The trouble is, union activists are forbidden from campaigning at work, while
management can spend all the time it wants at work campaigning against the union. Employees can be forced to
watch antiunion movies and submit to long meetings
where managers tell union horror stories to a single employee at a time, occasionally making threats that he'll be
fired if he votes for the union. Bosses have the names, ad-
dresses, and phone numbers of every employee, while
union activists have to find all that information out *without asking at work*. Most of this harassment is illegal, but
it's so hard to lodge a formal complaint with the National
Labor Relations Board, and the punishment is so light

(the fines are insignificant), that management almost always gets away with breaking the law.

Clearly unions need to reassess their purpose and strategy if they're to continue serving American workers with real force. It might be the innovations of Andy Stern, the president of the S.E.I.U. (Service Employees International Union)—the largest and fastest growing trade union in North America—that will revive unions in the United States. His ideas for consolidating unions, negotiating with whole industries and not just one company at a time, and working with unions overseas are controversial but gaining support among the rank and file. Unions are not an outdated idea; the corporate media may say they are, but workers know better. Union tactics just need to keep pace with the spread of multinational corporations.

We Americans have been told by government, media, and business leaders that we don't need unions; unions and even democracy itself, they say, won't make our lives better. The Market, they claim, will bring us everything we need, if we just work hard enough. The Market will take care of all our needs—from material comfort to social services. It sounds good on paper: free and fair competition on a level playing field will produce the best products at the cheapest prices. The Market even sounds democratic; the people buying the products will vote with their wallet for the best ones, paying more for things they value more, less for things they value less.

This myth of the market usually refers to an economy of hardworking small-business owners. Local businesses that sell the best product for a reasonable price with great customer service will succeed and expand. The myth crumbles, though, when you compare a small business with its real competition: large corporations that use tax shelters, outsource labor, collude with their competitors on pricing, and illegally bust unions. Companies like Wal-Mart have murdered small businesses, leaving ghost towns where there were once thriving commercial centers from Massachusetts to Virginia to Ohio and straight across the country. In place of the mom-and-pop store, we now have supermalls where most merchandise is made in China and most salespeople know and care nothing about what they sell.

Sound like a level playing field? Free and fair competition?

Members of Congress will talk about the "invisible hand of the market"—a hand that moves our economy with divine justice and compassion; a hand that guides society in the right direction. Ideologues like Newt Gingrich and George Bush have transformed Adam Smith's "invisible hand of the market" from a clever metaphor by a long-dead writer into an article of faith. Today's free-market activists take Smith at face value, but Smith, an eighteenth-century economist and philosopher, was writing about a world very different from ours. In *The Theory of Moral Sentiments*, for instance, he writes that "the rich . . . divide with the poor the produce of all their improvements. They are led by an invisible hand to make nearly the same distribution of the necessaries of life which would have been made, had the earth been divided into equal portions among all its inhabitants." Smith supported the equal distribution of goods, by these words, and would have fiercely opposed our current concentration of them in the hands of a few. His belief in the unfettered free-market system was intended to protect the farmers and artisans of his day, not twenty-first-century multinational corporations spread across the globe.

Smith believed domestic manufacturing and markets were the stability of a nation. While Congress and pundits treat his book *The Wealth of Nations* as the bible of free trade, it's clear that Smith would have opposed the WTO and IMF, NAFTA, and the World Bank, all of which shift our local economies offshore. Business, Smith believed, would stay home not for love of country, but because it was too risky to make or sell goods abroad: you couldn't watch over your employees, understand foreign laws, or trust intermediaries who had to literally carry products and cash around the world and back. Smith didn't calculate the greed that would arise from the invention of the telephone, Internet, airplane, and bank card machine; he couldn't foresee a day when it would be so easy to do business abroad that neither love of country nor fear of losses would keep businessmen in check.

The "invisible hand" is part of the catechism we're taught on how the economy works. Americans have come to view the free market as a religious mystery, a godlike force in the universe that can only be interpreted by the priesthood on Wall Street. The rest of us are to remain in our pews, obedient, unquestioning, and basking in our faith that a free market has the ability to solve all problems, right all wrongs.

But if the freest market is really the fairest, then how

do you explain poverty? How do you explain poverty if in a free market people are always rewarded for their effort, skill, and entrepreneurship? If free trade is our religion, then the only possible explanation for poverty is exactly the one we hear—that poor people are lazy, inherently inferior (women inferior to men, blacks inferior to whites, and so on). If wealth is the reward for hard work, then the poor must be poor because they're incapable of working hard, or unwilling to.

But poverty is not, of course, the result of laziness, gender, or skin color. It's the result of economic rules written to benefit the class of the people who wrote them. If the poor ran Congress, then Congress would write laws to benefit the poor. Instead, Congress writes laws that allow General Motors to leave for Mexico even though they're making huge profits manufacturing cars in the Midwest.

Economics is confusing and boring, soaked in jargon and impossible to question because the people on TV talking about the Dow and quarterly reports either don't make much sense or don't say anything useful to our daily lives. The stock market is reported on endlessly, but according to the Economic Policy Institute, the vast majority of Americans don't own stock. The bottom 80 percent of us collectively own only 10 percent of all the stock in the country. Yet stocks seem to dictate our lives anyway. Television and newspaper commentators are stock market junkies, reporting highs and lows as if our survival depended on them. At the same time, the market's practices have been called into question by some of its staunchest supporters. In 2002 Warren Buffett, who has made 36 billion dollars in the stock market, said he was "disgusted by the situation, so common in the last few years, in which shareholders have suffered billions in losses while the CEOs, promoters and other higher-ups who fathered these disasters have walked away with extraordinary wealth. . . . To their shame, these business leaders view shareholders as patsies, not partners."

If stock reports make most of us glaze over with boredom, recessions get our attention, plant closings get our attention, inflation gets our attention. The basic questions, though, go unasked: Who should decide how much money gets printed? Why should we give up our rights when we go to work? Why does a failing savings and loan get millions of dollars in free money to stay in business but not the deli around the corner?

There was a time when Americans asked questions about their economy. They studied it like a new car model to see if it was well made and safe and would take them where they wanted to go. Capitalism—the idea of an endless cycle where you start a business to make money, invest that capital in another business in order to make more money in order to start more businesses to make yet more money—is only about five hundred years old. The American economy, a hundred years ago, was not perceived as handed down with the apple to Adam and Eve; it was perceived as a human idea, as yet unproven. Questions were tossed around at town halls and union halls and populist meetings about who was benefiting and losing from the economy set up by our forefathers. Today we don't ask these questions. We ask what state our economy is in—whether the market is up or down—but not if it's badly designed in the first place and who it was designed for. Why, for instance, are unemployed single moms forced to "compete in the free market" with no welfare to help pay the bills, but Lockheed

Martin gets millions of dollars in welfare to stay in business?

The free market is, in fact, the last thing the corporate world wants. Our economy is designed to prevent competition among the rich and the corporate and require it for the rest of us. Businesses that would otherwise go under and fail in the marketplace are routinely "bailed out"; millions of dollars are taken from our pockets in the form of taxes and put into those of CEOs. In the 1980s, the Chrysler corporation would have gone out of business if it hadn't been for the federal government's handing it a check. If my house painting business goes under, I don't get a check from Washington to keep me afloat.

If there were really a level playing field, we would already have switched from nuclear to solar power, given that nuclear power is only cheap because of massive grants and subsidies from Washington.

There is no invisible hand. Like Dorothy in *The Wizard of Oz*, we need to pull back the curtain to see that there is no wizard; only Uncle Sam. Our economy is a product of human decisions and not the result of unknowable mystical forces moving the world in benevolent patterns that just happen to keep lavishing wealth on those born wealthy. The question, then, isn't should government interfere with business, since it already does; the question is, on whose behalf should government interfere?

In January 1994 the American government interfered on a huge scale on behalf of corporations. President Clinton signed into law the North American Free Trade Agreement (NAFTA), which removed or lowered tariffs to allow investment and manufacturing to move without restriction between Canada, the United States, and Mexico. NAFTA outlawed any local, state, or national laws that would get in the way of business. This treaty, negotiated behind closed doors and approved by the participating governments with little or no public discussion, literally put making money ahead of anything else these countries do. In practice, NAFTA means that corporations are free to pick up and leave their country for the country with the weakest environmental, worker protection, and consumer safety laws. That's why wildly profitable factories are leaving the United States and Canada for Mexico. With the introduction of newer free trade agreements with other countries around the world, those jobs are now leaving Mexico for places like China, where companies can make even more money by paying people even less. NAFTA and trade agreements like it—the Free Trade Area of the Americas (FTAA), the Central American Free Trade Agreement (CAFTA), and dozens of bilateral trade agreements between the United States and other countries—are a global race to the bottom. The bottom in terms of wages, the environment, human safety, and overall human rights.

For us here in America, NAFTA and other trade agreements created by Congress and unaccountable global organizations such as the WTO, the International Monetary Fund, and the World Bank have meant the devastation of American manufacturing and entire American towns. Flint, Michigan, made famous by Michael Moore's documentary *Roger and Me*, was only one of thousands of American cities and towns to be gutted by corporations who've moved their manufacturing onto foreign soil. American industry, on the whole, no longer bears any loyalty to a town and its workforce. A company will move in and put thousands of people to work, then leave years later to give those jobs to cheap laborers in Mexico. Businesses don't leave because times are tough and they need to find a solution or they'll go under—which, although it's still cruel, would be understandable. They leave when they're riding high and want to ride a little higher; this is the difference between self-interest and greed.

Perhaps most frightening of all, NAFTA has outright given a private corporation the power to overrule an independent government by suing it. Chapter 11 of NAFTA states that if a corporation thinks public policy is impeding its profits, it can sue that government to change its policy or pay a fine. The private American courier service UPS, for instance, has sued Canada for 160 million dollars in damages because it claims that Canada's publicly funded courier service has placed UPS at an unfair disadvantage. Suddenly corporations instead of officials elected by the populace are creating policy.

The creation of the World Trade Organization has been even more destructive than NAFTA. Before the WTO was approved in 1995, Ralph Nader put a challenge to the U.S. Congress. He pledged ten thousand dollars to the favorite charity of any member of Congress who would sign an affidavit that he had read the WTO agreement and would answer ten questions about it in public. No one took him up on it. So he extended the deadline by a week. Fifteen minutes before the deadline closed, Republican senator Hank Brown of Colorado called and accepted. A month later, Nader interrogated Brown in public about the trade agreement. Brown answered all twelve questions, but just before the interview ended, he said, "Wait. I have something to say. You know, I'm a free trader, and I voted for NAFTA, but after reading the WTO agreement, I was so appalled by the antidemocratic provisions that I'm going to vote against it and urge everyone else to." He didn't convince a single other senator.

Government and business have found superb tactics to bloat their bank accounts, and the fallout is nothing less than the dismantling of entire American communities. What countertactics can we use against them to save our livelihoods and, in many cases, our lives? As Arundhati Roy says, "It's enough of being right; now we need to win. . . . We need to . . . undo the nuts and bolts of empire."

* * *

In the search for our own tactics, there's no better place to start than the Zapatistas. In 1994, as NAFTA was being signed, the Zapatista Army of National Liberation left the Lacandon jungle to start a revolution in Mexico. Based in the southern state of Chiapas, the EZLN (Ejército Zapatista de Liberación Nacional) took several towns at gunpoint. Then they did something truly remarkable. They listened to the people they said they were fighting for. The Mexican people asked them to put down their weapons, and so for the last decade, the Zapatistas have held off the Mexican Army with words alone. Despite intimidation and massacres—like that at Acteal, where dozens of unarmed Zapatistas were shot by government troops—the Zapatistas have waged a war of words. They've used the Internet to create a network of mass communications that make it impossible for the Mexican Army to attack them secretly; at the same time, the network gives the revolutionaries a global platform from which to criticize the WTO and IMF policies that are suffocating Chiapas.

There are five Zapatista communities in southern Mexico, where the indigenous people run their communal life by consensus arrived at in meetings. They cooperatively run their farms and businesses, deciding for themselves how, where, and when they sell their farm produce, textiles, and crafts. There's a Zapatista brand of organic fair trade coffee, for instance, that's sold in restaurants and stores all over the world. The Zapatista communities are a living example of an alternative to undemocratic free trade practices.

If you own a business that must deal in foreign goods or use foreign labor, you could fight free trade abuses by using fair trade tactics. Check out "fair trade" on the Web to find how to employ humanely managed foreign workers or buy goods that are crafted under fair trade conditions. If you are a consumer of foreign goods— from coffee to textiles to soap—look for "fair trade" labels on your merchandise and buy the fair trade goods whenever possible over the generic, corporate brands. If it's a few cents or dollars more, consider buying less so you can buy better.

Another vital tactic we must use is to spread the truth about our economic realities in an age when the mainstream media tell one-half of every story: the corporate half. Ideally the media would reclaim its journalistic integrity and stop demonizing or slighting antiglobalization activists who, through mass demonstrations at

WTO and IMF meetings, expose our government's back-room dealings. In communications, the Zapatistas again have led the way. They have informed the world by way of the Internet about the real consequences of free trade by giving firsthand accounts. Their accounts are a kind of activist baton passed on to the global justice movement in a relay race for democracy. The goal is for everyone, not only the privileged, to decide his or her own destiny.

Another innovation in the democratic media came about during the massive Seattle protests of 1999. The global justice movement hit the evening news that November for shutting down the meeting of the WTO. While all the evening news reports parroted the Seattle police chief, who said his officers had fired into the crowd in self-defense, the activist-run Independent Media Center provided people with evidence that the police had fired rubber bullets point-blank at peaceful protestors. The IMC allowed anyone to post stories, pictures, video, and audio on a website dedicated to disseminating the facts.

One of the best tactics against free trade abuse is to coordinate protestors with delegates from developing countries who will be sitting down to negotiate with multinationals and banks. The meeting of the WTO and the IMF five months after Seattle's triumph is a perfect example. Tens of thousands of protestors outside gave "third world" delegates the leverage to wrestle millions of dollars in AIDS funding. In Mexico in 2003, the WTO's meeting was again aborted by a combination of demonstrations outside and protesting delegates inside. Our show of support for these poor countries gives them leverage and courage to not buckle under and to begin to make demands for worker rights, environmental protection, and humanitarian aid.

Corporations and the governments they control aren't all-powerful. Unions and popular movements have won decisive victories over the years. We don't often remember these victories, but the abolition of slavery, the minimum wage, the eight-hour day, progressive income taxes, and unemployment insurance have saved the lives and livelihoods of millions of people.

Of all the tools we have at our disposal, unions are the most powerful, even if they've been weakened since the height of their power in the 1930s and '40s. Strong unions are able to leverage concessions directly because they can threaten big business's ability to make money. A strong union's power to strike and grind business to a halt is the core of its power. By striking, it can force a business to obey the law and treat workers fairly; a union defends the rights and freedoms of us all, whether or not we're union members. Organizing and supporting unions may be the most important thing we can do to secure economic democracy.

But there are other projects that rack up economic victories on the side of the people.

In 2001 the City of Santa Monica, California, passed the country's most comprehensive living wage law. The law required businesses that make more than $5 million in annual gross revenues for at least two consecutive years to pay their employees $10.50 per hour—this in a state where the minimum wage was $6.25 and is now, as I write this in 2005, $6.75. While nearly fifty cities across the country have some form of living wage law, the law is limited to companies that do business with the municipality. Companies that pick up garbage, for instance, pay a living wage. The Santa Monica law, spearheaded on the city council by Green mayor Mike Feinstein and Green city councilmember Kevin McKeown, is the first in the country to enforce a living wage for private industry on private land.

The answer to our economic woes is not to go back in time at every turn for past solutions, but let's not throw out the proverbial baby with the bathwater either. Some parts of the New Deal, for example, make too much sense to ignore. Take the first minimum wage laws passed by New Deal congressmen as one tactic to pull the country out of the Depression and promote economic growth. Guaranteeing workers a minimum wage would mean they would have enough money not only to pay the bills but to spend in local stores, shoring up the small business owners who make up the bulk of the economy. If you have to scrape by just to pay the bills, you don't have money to go to the movies; then your local movie theater goes under for lack of customers and the people who worked there lose their jobs. Low wages create a spiral of job loss.

Living wage laws do what minimum wage law is no longer doing, because federal raises in the minimum wage don't come close to keeping pace with inflation. Minimum wage workers, despite incremental increases in their pay, make less and less money every year. Based on the value of today's dollars, the minimum wage in the early 1970s approached eight dollars an hour, compared with today's five or six. Washington's failure to provide a livable minimum wage has meant that local communities like Santa Monica have been forced to pick up the slack with their living wage laws.

As we organize our communities, gaining political power first at the local level, then with our state legislatures, we could use another tool that our legislatures fail to, the corporate death penalty. Corporations cannot currently do business without a charter from the state they want to do business in. For those companies that put our lives, jobs or environment at risk, the charter may be revoked.

Corporate charters are revoked all the time. But the state's Attorney General almost always targets small corporations; those that don't contribute millions of dollars to campaign accounts. New York State's Attorney General Eliot Spitzer even campaigned on charter revocation in 1998, saying, "when a corporation is convicted of repeated felonies that harm or endanger the lives of human beings or destroy our environment, the corporation should be put to death, its corporate existence ended, and its assets taken and sold at public auction." Spitzer has since made a name for himself prosecuting corporate crime, yet has almost always agreed to settle out of court. He gets headlines for himself this way, but does not force companies to even admit wrongdoing, let alone revoke their charters. What if state legislatures strengthened corporate charter laws to make corporations more accountable to the people? And what if state Attorneys General went after the GE's, Monsantos, and Lockheed Martins, putting them to death and selling their assets at public auction?

State legislatures already have the power to charter corporations, and in most states this has become a rubber-stamping process: a company fills out some paperwork, pays a fee, and it's incorporated, with all the attending rights and protections. But in the past, corporations were chartered for a specific purpose and a specific length of time. A corporation was chartered to, say, build a bridge, and when it was built, the corporation was dissolved. Now a corporation is chartered for things like "any legal purpose" and for a period of "indefinitely." Our state legislatures have the power to debate the public purpose of a corporate charter and require it to be task-specific and limited in time. The legislature simply chooses not to use its power to shape corporate enterprises into something beneficial or, at the very least, harmless to the public.

We need to use our local governments to institute new laws and strengthen old ones, as was done in Santa Monica. Get involved with your town council. As our local communities shore themselves up, they will gain the power to run themselves equitably.

The rich haven't always and won't always have this much power. Times change, empires fall. The only question is to what degree we will spend our lives extending their rule, and to what degree we'll spend our lives exploring ways to replace it.

CONCLUSION

Dare to Hope

Sins against hope are the only sins beyond forgiveness and redemption.

Eduardo Galeano

I don't have all the answers; no one does. While we still mourn the loss of the great leaders of the past—leaders like Dr. Martin Luther King, Jr. and César Chávez—we don't have time to wait for a new messiah. We live in a time of greater self-reliance, and we must take the lessons taught by everyone from Gandhi to Malcolm X and figure out how to use them on our own. We are the saviors we've been waiting for. The Zapatistas, with their revolution of words on the Web and their willingness to heed the will of the people, have begun the kind of democratic communal leadership that's needed. Let's follow their lead.

It's the realization that I don't know everything, don't

see every solution, that makes democracy so important to me. Discussion and debate are the lifeblood of a democratic nation. In a democracy, many voices speak—and more importantly, many voices are heard—so new solutions are always turning up, and we learn more than what we already know. But with only one voice speaking from two throats in Washington, the American people have been badgered into believing that only one exists, and its solution must be our only option. The truth of course is that there are as many answers as there are cultures and opinions in this country, and Americans must learn to listen to them all and learn from them all. Fundamentalism is the fruit of a society whose avenues for meaningful debate have been closed.

Proportional representation and a multiparty democracy aren't exactly sexy solutions but they're desperately needed. They're the perfect vehicle to make sure that more voices are heard. Only one in one hundred U.S. senators is black, while 12.9 percent of the American people are: Barack Obama is only the fifth black senator in U.S. history. There are only fourteen female senators, though just over half of the American people are women. There have only ever been thirty-three women senators in American history—1.76 percent of all who have served in the Senate. That's not to mention the innumerable other constituencies that go unrepresented and unheard, whose issues go undebated. The most powerful decision-making bodies in the country are swollen with straight white men like me. Unlike me, nearly all the straight white men who come to power are rich. They do not represent the needs and will of our nation.

*   *   *

For some, the way to achieve democracy is to take to the streets and topple the imperialist American regime and reorganize the global economy. For others, it's to work out a compromise and build the trust of the opposition; those who trust you will listen to you harder and one day come around. It can't be one cure or the other. If we're going to uproot America's free-market ideology and replace it with a humane vision of progress, we need to use whatever tactic suits the situation at hand. We need to be radical at times, cautious at others; fierce at times, gentle at others. A hammer alone won't build a house; you need all the tools in the box.

Democrats have destroyed themselves by not understanding this. Twenty years ago, they chose to wield one single tool: to be more like their opponent. For twenty years, faced with Republican victories, the Democrats have chosen to weaken their message and adopt Republican issues. When conservatives, on the other hand, realized the country was against them in the 1960s, they didn't lie down and give up; they fought like hell to persuade and coerce the country until the country agreed with them. The conservative movement's response to Senator Barry Goldwater's defeat in the 1964 presidential election was to start planning how it would win the country back on its own terms. Republicans didn't see Lyndon Johnson's landslide victory as a sign that they needed to soften their message, cave in to working-class issues, and become more like Democrats. Conservatives instead decided what they wanted and became supreme at getting it through political organizing and winning elections. They founded hundreds of think tanks like the Heritage Foundation, bought up and created media empires like Fox News, and groomed candidates, such as Ronald Reagan, who would vote conservative but present themselves as all-American.

Along the way, Republican financiers forged alliances with the evangelical Christian movement. Preaching God's will to the poor instead of offering health benefits and a decent minimum wage worked: while the secular social service budget has been mercilessly slashed, churches have begun to pick up the slack. In too many cities across the country, the only place for the unemployed to get a warm bed and a hot meal is the basement of an evangelical church. The clergy get fuller pews and government checks for their "faith-based initiatives," and faith becomes a prerequisite for a full belly. The Republicans made their comeback by putting religion at the service of finance, and finance at the service of religion. The fundamentalist churches got rich and the financiers that hooked up with them got rich. The only ones who haven't gotten rich are the majority of Americans who work for a living.

The opposite approaches of the Democrats and Republicans can be seen all too clearly on the issue of abortion. After George W. Bush's election in 2004, both parties began to maneuver for position. Republican senator Arlen Specter was next in line to chair the Senate Judiciary Committee, in charge of reviewing presidential appointments to the federal courts. When Specter said, in passing, that it would be unlikely for the Senate to approve a pro-life nominee to the Supreme Court, the Republican leadership was furious. Unless Specter retracted his statement, the Republicans threatened to break Senate rules and tradition and deny him the chairmanship. So Specter announced that the fact that he was personally pro-choice did not mean he would work to appoint a pro-choice justice to the Supreme Court. His leash had been pulled hard and he did what he was told; the Republican Party agenda held fast.

The Democrats likewise began to position themselves on abortion. Faced with the defeat of Senate leader Tom Daschle, Senate Democrats had to elect someone new. They chose Senator Harry Reid, a *pro-life* Democrat. Their choice sent a clear signal to the country that, like Arlen Specter, Senate Democrats wouldn't let their pro-choice stand get in the way of appointing another pro-life Supreme Court justice. The *Daily Show*'s Jon Stewart might have been referring to the whole Democratic Party when he impersonated Specter by yelling, "Come *on*! Just because I have convictions doesn't mean I'm gonna *stand* by 'em!" If Specter didn't stand by his convictions, the Republicans sure did. The Democrats, by contrast, abandoned a cause that has helped define their party for a generation.

Likewise, Democratic support groups around the country have backed down on core issues. The Human Rights Campaign—the largest gay, lesbian, bisexual, and transgender organization in the country—publicly stated their intention to soften their message and not ask for as much as they had in the past.

For generations, the Democratic Party's domestic policy was organized around economic issues: the New Deal, the Great Society, civil rights. Rather than develop innovative programs based on the same values, the Democrats have for thirty years abandoned the fight on behalf of the poor, choosing instead to join the Republicans in designing an economy that helps those who need no help. Betraying those who relied on you is good strategy, say Democratic leaders. After all, the poor can't contribute nearly as much to campaigns as the rich. With no populist economic policies to inspire and mobilize people, with neither major party helping to put food on the table, elections are won or lost on social issues. With issues like the economy and war beyond debate, the differences between

Democrats and Republicans narrow into small disagreements over a handful of major issues like gay marriage and abortion. The bottom line is that the Republican Party leadership has solid convictions and the Democratic Party leadership doesn't. Right or wrong, people respond to convictions. They know where you stand on an issue and know you'll fight for what you believe in. No one respects a politican without conviction. Faced with a choice between a candidate who'll screw them with conviction and one who'll screw them for political gain, most Americans won't vote. The ones who do will more likely vote for the candidate with conviction.

If you're not happy with the Republican agenda of economic irresponsibility, warmongering, environmental destruction, and privatized health care and Social Security, how could you be happy with the Democratic agenda of economic irresponsibility, warmongering, environmental destruction, and privatized health care and Social Security? When we're told we need to swallow our convictions and do something that betrays our principles, we need to say no. What are principles and convictions for except to guide our actions? If we begin to guide our actions by what we're told will work, as opposed to what we believe in, there is no way we are going in the right direction. As progressives, we need to ask ourselves not what sort of Democrat should we be—radical, moderate, or meek— but what sort of person we should be, and act accordingly. Organize and vote Green, or invent a new party. There are other options than the two-party system strangling our democracy.

* * *

It's in our power to topple the people who would kill us for money. But politicians, the media, and our educational system have convinced us we're powerless. We're like elephants at the circus: they're strong enough to walk away, but they've been convinced since they were little that there's no point in trying. When baby elephants join the circus, a huge chain is put around their ankle that binds them to a stake. For years they pull and yank at that chain, trying to get away, and eventually give up. After years of failing, adult elephants come to believe they can't escape, no matter how hard they try. When full grown, they can be kept prisoner with just a thin rope tying them to that stake. Though the grown elephant is more than strong enough to snap the rope, the memory of the chain keeps him from even trying. We have to stop believing we can't break that rope.

Hope is a tricky word. It's been exhausted by preachers and politicians as a quick fix for suffering. But that kind of hope is passive; it means you just wait around, hoping things will get better. I'm interested in a more active hope, one rooted in the memories of our past victories, one based on the understanding that change happens all the time all around us. Change is not only possible but inevitable, and it's directed by those willing to fight relentlessly for what they believe in.

The results of our actions for peace and democracy aren't always immediately visible; sometimes they happen much later, sometimes in places or for people we didn't expect. We need to rejoice in our small victories, not just wait for the massive public events—the two million people marching for peace, the all-star concert for women's rights. We need to pull away from what writer Rebecca Solnit calls "the anesthetizing distractions of this society" to become politically aware and active now and continually. We need hope if we're going to disobey the government when it puts us in danger. Instead of complacently allowing America to die with a whimper at the hands of people Mussolini would have gotten along fine with, every decent American should be fighting tooth and nail to preserve the vision of America we all learned about in grade school.

Eduardo Galeano's words bear repeating: "Utopia is on the horizon. When I walk two steps, it takes two steps back. I walk ten steps and it is ten steps further away. What is utopia for? It is for this, for walking." Rather than give up and stop walking, rather than kick and scream that a perfect world doesn't fall into our laps just because we want it to, we need to learn how to walk—trusting our passion and our convictions to guide us to a better world.

Acknowledgments

Thanks to those who were happy for me when I liked how the book was coming, and were patient enough to deal with my complaining when I wasn't; Colin Apse, April Daly, Nancy and Larry Caban, Jim Gordon, Sarah Hoop, Paul Maloney, Lyndon Roeller, Rebecca Rotzler, Nora Strano, Ben Vis, Jenny Vis, Jonathan Wright, Lilah Weiss, Ron West, Amanda West, and Michael Zierler.

Thanks to Billiam van Roestenberg, Jeff McGowan, and Ian Kleinert for persuading me to write a book and convincing me it was possible.

Thanks to the amazingly patient people at Miramax, for having faith in a first-time author and for bending over backwards to help me when I needed it: Jonathan Burnham, Kristin Powers, and my editor JillEllyn Riley.

Thanks to Rebecca Rotzler and Michael Zierler for being politicians who follow their convictions and for being people I've been proud to serve with.

Thanks to the the friends who read parts of the manuscript, offered advice, helped me sort out tangled thoughts, and offered criticism I obsessed over and compliments I didn't believe; Pinar Batur, Ed Felton, Jim Gordon, Eamon Martin, David Rovics, John Vanderlippe, Lilah Weiss, and Ron West.

And thanks to Susan Bell, for the editorial and writing skills that pulled this book together and for stoically being dragged past deadline after deadline.